THE HISTOR
HOLLYWOOD

THE HISTORY OF HOLLYWOOD

A CENTURY OF GREED, CORRUPTION, AND SCANDAL BEHIND THE MOVIES

KIERON CONNOLLY

amber
BOOKS

This revised paperback edition first published in 2023

First published in 2014

Copyright © 2023 Amber Books Ltd

Published by
Amber Books Ltd
United House
North Road
London
N7 9DP
United Kingdom
www.amberbooks.co.uk
Facebook: amberbooks
Twitter: @amberbooks
Pinterest: amberbooksltd

Project Editor: Sarah Uttridge
Designer: Zoë Mellors
Picture Research: Terry Forshaw

ISBN: 978-1-83886-278-7

Printed in United States

CONTENTS

INTRODUCTION

If Hollywood, with its pepper trees, orange and avocado gardens, bougainvillea vines and warm, sunny climate, had seemed like the Garden of Eden to the first film-makers when they arrived in California in the early 1910s, cinema must have brought the serpent with it.

◆

'A town with all the personality of a paper cup.'

A century after the founding of Hollywood, we find in the movie studios and mansions a history of greed, corruption and cover-ups, of overdoses, suicides and sexual abuse, of, at the very least, licentiousness and hypocrisy, and, at the worst, murder. For a town where a hundred years ago too much sun probably seemed the greatest harm one could do to oneself, much has changed.

While a heady mix of wealth, power and ambition has always been the oxygen that fuels Tinseltown, the industry doesn't simply attract pretty people in search of fame, it *requires* them. And, like a fairytale, the lives

To outsiders, Hollywood can seem like El Dorado, but, as Raymond Chandler wrote about those who have succeeded to the inside, 'there's the constant fear of losing all this fairy gold and being the nothing they have really never ceased to be'.

of those so blessed can be radically remoulded in chance happenings: Jean Harlow was first seen in a Hollywood car park, while Lana Turner, having slipped out of a high-school typing class, really was discovered in a Sunset Strip ice-cream parlour. When fame arrives like that, especially when such luck is involved, it has to be at least a little unsettling.

Follow the American Dream and Archie Leach can be reinvented as Cary Grant, Thomas Mapother can become Tom Cruise, while hair colour and even faces can be changed to create Marilyn Monroe and Rita Hayworth. Success, however, especially in Tinseltown, can be fickle. Hollywood might not sneer at someone's origins, but nor does it care what happens once their moment has passed. As an industry town, it is snobbish only about career status. 'The guest lists of the highly publicized big parties reeked of it,' wrote English actor David Niven. 'The successful and established were invited; the struggling and the passé were not.'

And for those who never become successful, it has always been a cruel place. Even in the early years,

Above: Orson Welles, in the wheelchair, directing *Citizen Kane*. Cinema is a peculiar art form: it's delicate, but mass-produced, artistic but has no sole artist. And for a century Hollywood has been its most successful peddler of dreams to millions of people around the world.

unemployed actors were known to walk around town in heavy greasepaint, hoping to create the impression that they were working in the Dream Factory.

But for those who *did* make it and did last, it must surely have been wonderful, mustn't it? Maybe not. 'There was nothing to recommend this town at all,' said actress Nina Foch, who began working in movies in the late 1940s. 'There was nothing cultivated about it anywhere. It was filled with brown bodies and brown minds.' In fact, while the industry was busy crafting some beautiful movies to charm the world, it seemingly did little else of worth, beyond creating wealth for itself. 'It was a hotbed of false values,' wrote David Niven. 'It harboured an unattractive percentage of small-time crooks and con artists.'

Yet it's that mix between the creative moment on-screen and the hugely commercial industry around

'It's the only manufacturing business,' wrote screenwriter William Ludwig, 'where the capital assets go home at 5.30pm.'

it, between the delicate and the mass-produced, that generates our fascination with Hollywood. A seemingly private lovers' kiss on camera, filmed in front of a large film crew, can touch audiences in thousands of cinemas around the world.

Altogether cinema is a peculiar art form. It is artistic, but there's no sole artist. It's creative, but it can be immensely expensive. As Orson Welles said: 'A writer needs a pen, an artist needs a brush, but a film-maker needs an army.' This creates unusual problems and Hollywood, as, financially, the world's largest film industry, has the most extreme examples. 'It's the only manufacturing business,' wrote screenwriter William Ludwig, 'where the capital assets go home at 5.30pm, where they can get drunk, where they can get killed. That can't happen in an automobile plant; the presses don't go home, the steel doesn't get drunk.'

Those assets are, of course, the stars who on-screen look beautiful and heroic, always ready with the right quip and the winning smile, as we laugh and cry with them before their stories are resolved, usually happily. And even though we know they're only playing a part, we identify with them, fall in love with them a little and perhaps even entertain the thought that we might like to meet them one day. *Dark History of Hollywood* could just put us off that fantasy. It's a question of how much we really want to know.

'People in the East pretend to be interested in how pictures are made,' F. Scott Fitzgerald wrote about Hollywood. 'But if you actually tell them anything, you find … they never see the ventriloquist for the doll.' Beguiled by its glamour, Fitzgerald's friends had no interest beyond the 'pretensions, extravagances and vulgarities' of Tinseltown. There's nothing wrong with that, and there's plenty of it in *Dark History of Hollywood*. But there's also a fuller story to be told on how Hollywood came to be, how it survived and how it still operates today.

> 'We don't go for strangers in Hollywood … we tell them lies so well rehearsed even we don't always recall if they're true.'

Not that it's always willing to offer us the truth. 'We don't go for strangers in Hollywood,' said Fitzgerald's narrator in his novel *The Last Tycoon*, 'and when we do, we tell them lies so well rehearsed even we don't always recall if they're true.' In a town rich in and rich from story-tellers, Hollywood fact has to be separated from Hollywood fiction.

Dark History of Hollywood uncovers the true stories of Tinseltown, as it reveals where the power lies, shows how the film industry really works, and, in so doing, exposes the ventriloquist behind the doll.

Below: An audience watching a 3-D film in 1952. The Lumière brothers first projected moving pictures before an audience in 1894, but, years later, Louis Lumière said: 'Had I been able to foresee what cinema would become, I'd never have invented it'.

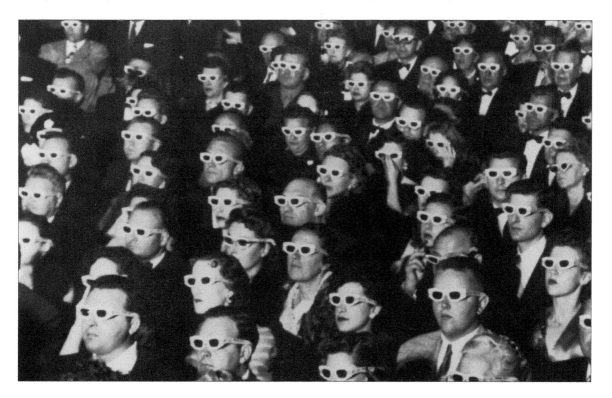

Edison

PHOTO PLAY

NOW BEING PERFORMED

FOUNDING FATHERS

In 1908, America's cultural life, including its film-making, was led from New York, and France had the world's largest film industry. So how was it that by 1919 Hollywood had become not only the centre of film-making in the United States but also the largest force for movies around the world? As well as hard work and good luck, it's a story that involves bootlegging, theft, piracy, cartels and violence.

◆

'Cinema has no commercial value. At most, it'll last a year.'

Cinema wasn't conceived in Hollywood, but some would argue that it was born in America. In 1896, the cinématographe, invented by Antoine Lumière and his sons Louis and Auguste, was presented in New York. While earlier inventions had been more like slot machines where a single viewer looked through a peep hole, the cinématographe was the first projector to throw light and shadows on a wall and offer moving images to a mass audience. Quickly

Part of the appeal of early silent cinema was that the audience didn't need to be literate or even be able to speak English. They spoke the universal language of visual images, 'the Esperanto of the Eye', as one writer called it.

the cinématographe, which gives us the word 'cinema', proved a success around the world – so much so that within a year it had been studied and improved upon by other moving-picture inventors.

But, as the movie business now knows well, where there's a hit, there's a writ. No sooner had the Lumières demonstrated their invention than Thomas Edison, inventor of the light bulb, the phonograph and the ticker-tape machine, as well as being a busy litigator, stepped in. Claiming that he'd created a device for viewing moving pictures five years earlier, he went to court, alleging that *all* other machines were infringing his patent – this despite the more recent inventions being far more sophisticated and the fact that Edison's machine itself owed a great deal to the earlier work of Étienne Jules Marey. The battle for who owned cinema had begun, and it wasn't a battle fought only in the courts – Edison's lawsuit against American Mutoscope

SEATS FOR THE FUNERAL

WHEN SAM, HARRY and Albert Warner – the three elder Warner Brothers – opened their first nickelodeon in Pennsylvania in 1905, they used chairs from the funeral parlour next door. If they had a very popular film showing, a funeral service would have to be postponed while they borrowed the chairs. And if the undertaker had a large service, they'd delay the start of their film until the chairs were available.

Harry Warner (centre), with Albert (right) and fourth brother Jack (left) in 1965.

> While the lawsuits were making their way through the legal process, cameras could be rented, bought or stolen …

(later the Biograph Company) lasted for ten years and even lead to street fights. But while the lawsuits were making their way through the legal process, cameras could be rented, bought or stolen – the bootlegging of equipment and even finished films being common.

With films proving relatively inexpensive to make, offering returns that could be very high, one early commentator said: 'All you needed was fifty dollars, a broad and a camera.' With that, a short, silent vaudeville act could be put on film.

As movies were at first basically a fairground attraction, another observer correctly described the people involved in them as a 'collection of former carnival men, ex-saloon keepers, medicine men, concessionaires of circus side shows, photographers and peddlers'. Cinema was cheap entertainment

aimed not at the well-off but the urban poor, with the result that initially cultured and professional financiers missed out.

Others, however, saw the possibilities. And as cinema became more successful, more permanent homes for screening films sprang up in disused shops and theatres in America's slum districts. These venues were called 'nickelodeons', a clever mix of the cheap and the grand: the cost of admission was a nickel (5 cents), while 'odeon' was Ancient Greek for a building where musical performances were held.

Nickel Delirium

The beauty of silent films was that they could be enjoyed by new immigrants without fluent English, the way theatre and even vaudeville could not. And almost everyone was welcome at a nickelodeon. Unlike restaurants, vaudeville or social clubs, no one was barred from a nickelodeon on account of gender or religion, or, with some exceptions, race (although

Right: Charles Pathé began in business with a phonograph stall at French fairgrounds, before turning his attention to the mass production of movies. 'I didn't invent cinema,' he said, 'but I did industrialize it.'

Offering everyone the chance
to sit privately but in public,
a woman could go to a nickelodeon
without an escort.

in many US states nickelodeons were segregated). Offering everyone the chance to sit privately but in public, a woman could go to a nickelodeon without an escort and without being the focus of unwanted attention. The most popular genres were comedies and thrillers, and few films lasted more than 25 minutes.

It's estimated that by 1907 there were more than 4000 nickelodeons across America, each of them offering 12 shows a day, with 200,000 people a day going to the movies in New York alone. The number doubled on Sundays.

But although nickelodeons were quickly booming across America, it was the French company Pathé that was making the most films. Completing one short film every day by 1908, Pathé was producing silent fantasies, biblical stories and melodramas, and soon opened offices in Bombay, Singapore and Melbourne to supervise their distribution. America wasn't even the second largest film-producing country – Denmark was, with Copenhagen-based Nordisk large enough to employ 2000 people in an industry that was barely a few years old.

But when Charles Pathé complained that Edison was pirating copies of his films for US release, Edison responded by issuing Pathé with a writ. Trying to hold

… when legal channels didn't work
swiftly enough, Edison turned
heavy, hiring private detectives and
thugs to harass his competitors …

on to what he perceived as his intellectual copyright over cinema, Edison issued lawsuits alleging that film companies and cinemas not using his equipment were infringing his patent on cameras and projectors. And when legal channels didn't work swiftly enough, Edison turned heavy, hiring private detectives and thugs to

harass his competitors as they were actually filming. Although some rivals quickly set up decoy film crews to occupy the detectives, while the genuine crew worked undisturbed elsewhere, eventually, through channels legal or otherwise, Edison managed to hound many companies out of business.

The Arrival of the Moguls

It wasn't long before the success of cinema began to attract a new generation of entrepreneurs. They weren't well educated and they weren't scientists or inventors, like Edison or the Lumières, but they were determined and had a keen eye on the market. They were Jewish immigrants from Europe, who were seeking a better life in North America: Samuel Goldwyn was from Warsaw, Adolph Zukor (one of the founders of Paramount Pictures) and William Fox (whose company merged to form 20th Century Fox) were Hungarian, while Carl Laemmle (of Universal Pictures) was from Germany. All moved to the US as teenagers. Louis B. Mayer (later of Metro-Goldwyn-Mayer), who was from Minsk, Belarus, moved to the US as a toddler and three of the four Warner brothers moved from Poland as children. All of them worked their way up in other forms of business: Goldwyn became a master glove salesman, Zukor was in furs, Fox was in the garment trade, Mayer in scrap metal and the Warners struggled through various modest ventures, including a bicycle shop. In Hollywood style, their lives would become rags-to-riches stories. With most of them having done well in their respective businesses, they would succeed in resisting Edison's attempts to monopolize the new medium.

Risking losing control of the film business to these new, independent nickelodeon entrepreneurs, Edison and his main competitors at American Mutoscope and Biograph Company (AM&B), agreed in 1908 to settle their differences and create a cartel to keep the upstarts out. In this they tried to monopolize the cameras and projectors that made film-making possible. Titled The Motion Picture Patents Company (MPPC), competitors quickly referred to the cartel as 'The Trust'.

By limiting the number of companies allowed to use its film stock, cameras and projectors, the Trust

Right: Thomas Edison tried to dominate movies by controlling the use of his inventions – cameras, projectors and film stock. The more commercially minded understood that the money in cinema was actually in making and distributing films.

Above: Carl Laemmle, the founder of Universal, with his children
Rosabelle and Carl Jr. Laemmle, whose named is pronounced 'lem-
lee', was known for employing his relatives – as Ogden Nash rhymed:
'Uncle Carl Laemmle, has a very large faemmle.'

barred many US and all but two overseas producing
companies, one being Pathé. Before the Trust's
measures were put into action, foreign films had
made up more than two-thirds of the total number of
films released in America, but within a year that figure
had halved. The European film industry, which had
come to rely on America as its largest export market,
was never as powerful again. By limiting foreign
imports, the Trust had muscled its way to the top of
American cinema.

> At a time when women in most
> US states didn't even have the vote,
> Pickford was able to choose her
> co-stars and directors.

Cinema's First Stars

Universal's Carl Laemmle only managed to abide by
the Trust's terms for three months before he rebelled,
putting an advertisement in the trade press: 'I Have Quit
The Patents Company ... No More Licenses! No More
Heartbreaks!' To meet the demand of supplying cinemas
with non-Trust films, however, Laemmle realized he'd

have to start making movies himself. Renting space in New York, he launched his own studio and set about looking for talent to put in front of the camera.

Many actors and actresses were already tied into long-term contracts with the Trust companies, which deliberately didn't name them, rightly suspecting that if they did, they'd become the attraction and would begin demanding higher fees. For this reason, Biograph's Florence Lawrence was known only as 'the Biograph

---

> At one point, Laemmle even moved his company to Cuba, but still found mysterious 'tourists' busying themselves photographing the company's equipment …

Girl', while Mary Pickford was 'The Girl with the Curls'.

When Laemmle managed to poach Lawrence and Pickford from Biograph in 1909 and they began working under their usual stage names, Pickford's weekly salary climbed from $175 to $10,000, with a yearly bonus of $300,000. At a time when women in most US states didn't even have the vote, Pickford was able to choose her co-stars and directors. Movie acting, for a select few, rapidly became the highest paid profession in the world.

Not that the Trust had given up trying to police the use of cameras. At one point, Laemmle even moved his company to Cuba, but still found mysterious 'tourists' busying themselves photographing the company's equipment rather than Mary Pickford. Attempts were also made to discredit the independents. 'How can an ex-huckster, ex-bellboy, ex-tailor, ex-advertising man, ex-bookmaker know anything about picture quality?' ran an editorial in the trade paper *Moving Picture World*. 'Hands that would be more properly employed with a push cart on the lower East Side are responsible for directing stage plays and making pictures of them.'

Then, in 1910, when the Trust began an attempt to control distribution and William Fox refused, it bribed an exhibitor to screen some of Fox's films in a brothel,

Right: At first, Mary Pickford's studio billed her as 'The Girl with the Curls', correctly anticipating that if she was named she'd become a star and would demand more money and special treatment.

**Left: A 1909 advertisement in trade newspaper *Moving Picture World*
calling for companies to break away from the restrictions of Edison's
Trust and work independently.**

**Above: An 1887 estate agent's map of Hollywood land for development.
Hollywood film-makers first encountered an area renowned for its
balmy orange and avocado gardens.**

thus giving the Trust grounds to cancel his licence.
Infuriated, Fox encouraged the government to bring a
Federal suit against the Trust. It was the beginning of
the end for Edison's control over cinema. And when, in
1912, Laemmle won a legal victory over the Trust, the
independents were free to use any camera they chose.

At the end of that year, the US government issued an
anti-competitive suit against the Trust, but by then
Laemmle, Fox and Zukor were already succeeding
despite the Trust's demands. The Trust had been
broken: that year half of American films were made by
independents. In 1918, it was formally dissolved.

WHY IS IT CALLED 'HOLLYWOOD'?

DAEIDA HARTELL WILCOX Beveridge and her husband,
Harvey Wilcox, moved to southern California in 1886
and bought 200 acres of apricot and fig groves near Los
Angeles at the cost of $150 an acre. While travelling
by train to visit family in her hometown in Hicksville,
Ohio, Daeida met a woman from the Chicago area,

who lived on a country estate that she referred to
as 'Hollywood'. Liking the name, Daeida gave it to
her new California ranch. After Wilcox failed at fruit
farming, the couple divided the property into lots to
sell them off. By 1910, when the film-makers began to
arrive, Hollywood still had a population of only 166.

A BARN IN HOLLYWOOD

CECIL B. DEMILLE, in 1913, had been preparing to film a Western, *The Squaw Man*. Until then many Westerns had been made way out west... west New Jersey, but DeMille was going to be shooting in winter and New Jersey wouldn't do, so they settled on Arizona. DeMille, his crew of three and one actor left by train from New York. After two days, they reached Flagstaff, Arizona, but a snowstorm was raging. They quickly reboarded the train and carried on to Los Angeles, knowing that other crews had made short films there in the winter and that there were laboratories to process the film.

From LA, they sent back a telegram to New York: 'FLAGSTAFF NO GOOD FOR OUR PURPOSE, HAVE PROCEEDED TO CALIFORNIA. WANT AUTHORITY TO RENT BARN IN PLACE CALLED HOLLYWOOD.' The barn cost $75 a month. Sam Goldwyn, their financial backer, authorized the rent, stating, 'DON'T MAKE ANY LONG COMMITMENT.' Goldwyn subsequently moved to Los Angeles and made films there for the next 40 years.

Way out West

So why did film-makers leave cultured New York, with its Broadway actors at hand, cross the country and re-establish themselves in southern California? There are several reasons. In the early days of cinema, all scenes, whether interiors or exteriors, were filmed outside. With interiors of film sets having no ceilings, sunlight was used to light a scene, and if the weather clouded over, filming stopped. With its very bright light and warm, even climate, California was perfect for film-makers. And Los Angeles in particular, situated between the ocean and the desert, with the Santa Monica Mountains as a backdrop, offered a wide range of exterior locations. Also, land was less expensive there and, as Los Angeles was still the country's main non-unionized city, labour was cheaper, too.

Then there was the boom city of Los Angeles itself. In 1850, the whole LA area from coast to desert had a population of only around 2500 people. By 1890 about 150,000 people lived there. What had happened in between? In the 1870s and 1880s, the railroad had opened up the Los Angeles basin. LA could now be reached in five days from New York. And, as an incentive to move west, fares were cheap: $1 for a train ticket from Kansas City to LA. And when in 1892 oil was discovered in Los Angeles, the city became a place of opportunity for new ventures.

But there was one more reason, too: LA was 3000 miles from the harassment of the Trust. Not that the Trust didn't follow the film-makers to California.

'Every now and then I would see him standing on a rise watching us through field glasses,' wrote producer Fred J. Balshofer of his experiences in 1910 with Trust detective Al McCoy. 'Whenever I spotted him, I'd send one of the cowboys riding in his direction with instructions just to inquire who he was, but McCoy would always disappear before the rider reached him.'

Balshofer thought he'd seen the back of McCoy, but becoming aware of a break-in at his office one night, he and a colleague, George Gebhardt, armed with a pistol, approached the building. 'Gebhardt jammed the gun into the man's back and barked "Hands up!"' he recalled. The man dropped a package to the floor and begged them not to shoot. It was their own camera boy, who'd been persuaded by McCoy to take photographs of their Pathé camera. After that Balshofer wrapped the camera in a Navajo blanket and stored it in a bank vault every night. Then, when subpoenaed by the Trust, he removed it before they could place a court order to open up the bank vault. In this way, he managed to complete his film.

The Trust was fighting a losing battle. But even after it had lost control of the copyright on cameras, it still tried to protect the short films that its companies made.

The Squaw Man was the first feature-length movie made in Hollywood and its makers were wary of the

Right: The first feature film made in Hollywood, *The Squaw Man* (1914) tells the story of an English aristocrat in the Wild West who scandalously falls in love with a Native American.

Trust's interference. 'They were making easy money with little effort on short films,' wrote its producer Jesse L. Lasky of the Trust. 'They were afraid longer films would ruin the whole business by driving patrons out of the theatres with eyestrain and boredom – or, worse still, the public might get to like long pictures and force the film-makers to worry about heavier financing and genuine creative talent.'

Quite literally, the Trust was missing the bigger picture. Adolph Zukor had recognized that while the Trust was busy with litigation, its audience was becoming bored by its product. Longer films with more complex stories were needed. The first film Zukor distributed was a 52-minute French movie about the love affairs of Queen Elizabeth I of England, while the first film he produced was an adaptation of the novel *The Prisoner of Zenda*.

Don't Come Knocking

Today, Hollywood may be the home of American cinema, but initially film-makers found themselves unwelcome. Rooming houses, aware of the rumours about debauched show business folk, left signs in their windows reading, 'No dogs! No actors!'

> Rooming houses, aware of the rumours about debauched show business folk, left signs reading, 'No dogs! No actors!'

Agnes DeMille, niece of director Cecil B. DeMille, remembered that before the film-makers arrived, Hollywood was populated 'by citizens of the Middle West who had come to the Coast to die at ease in the sun'. The existing population of farmers, early oil tycoons and estate agents regarded the 'movie colony' as a passing fad. Hollywood's elite has now come to own some of the most expensive properties around LA, but back then, as Agnes DeMille wrote, 'The contempt of the real estate operator for the movie was without blemish; it was his one perfect characteristic.'

Below: Opened by Carl Laemmle in 1915, Universal City Studio wasn't situated in Hollywood itself because no one there would sell to the film-maker. Instead, he built his studio just over the Santa Monica Mountains in the San Fernando Valley.

BIRTH OF A NATION

D.W. GRIFFITH'S *BIRTH of a Nation* (1915) has the mixed honour of being not only a hit film, and the first movie to be regarded as serious entertainment, but also as being responsible for a revival in the Ku Klux Klan. Portraying the period around the American Civil War as an assault on the dignity of the South and the virtue of its women by black-loving Northerners and African-Americans (played by white actors in blackface), it characterizes the Ku Klux Klan as a heroic force that was restoring order. African-Americans for their part are depicted as stupid, vindictive and sexually aggressive. Perhaps not surprisingly, the film provoked protest from the NAACP (National Association for the Advancement of Coloured People) and white liberals, and led to riots in Boston and, it is believed, 22 lynchings in Georgia in the year it was released. There was even a ten-year surge in Klan membership, which reached eight million. The film, though frequently banned, was shown widely and became the highest-grossing film ever until another Civil War epic, *Gone with the Wind*, was released 24 years later.

The controversy around the film would have a long-lasting consequence within Hollywood cinema. After *Birth of a Nation*, rather than upset anyone with positive or negative depictions of African-Americans, Hollywood simply omitted them altogether or relegated them to weak supporting roles as clowns, singers, dancers and servants. With a few exceptions, African-American characters became notable by their absence for three decades of Hollywood cinema.

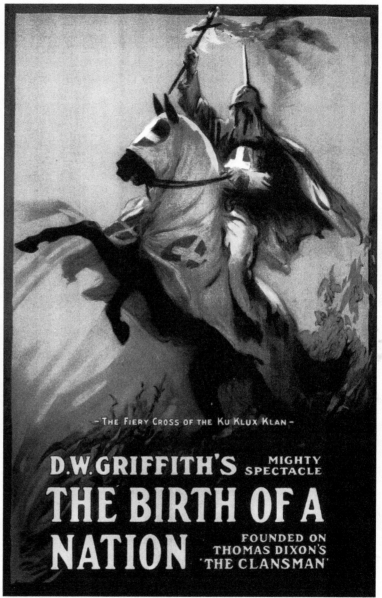

– THE FIERY CROSS OF THE KU KLUX KLAN –

D.W. GRIFFITH'S MIGHTY SPECTACLE
THE BIRTH OF A NATION
FOUNDED ON THOMAS DIXON'S 'THE CLANSMAN'

Left: Lillian Gish in *Birth of a Nation*. It was the most expensive movie of its time and, although its triumphant portrayal of the Ku Klux Klan was controversial, it became a major hit.

Altogether, old Hollywood could be actively hostile to film-makers. Cecil B. DeMille was shot at twice by angry residents while filming *The Squaw Man*, and, after the first negative of the film was sabotaged, he began sleeping in the film lab to protect his copy of the movie.

Despite their frosty reception from the Los Angeles population, the first Hollywood studio entrepreneurs were not to be deterred. And when, in 1914, Carl Laemmle found no one would sell him land in Hollywood, he bought a 230-acre ranch on the other side of the Santa Monica Mountains in the San Fernando Valley – and began building a giant studio there: Universal. A year later, 200 Universal employees boarded a special train from New York to take them to their new jobs in southern California. On arriving in Los Angeles after the hot Midwest plains, one traveller described it as 'like coming out of an inferno into paradise'.

Fortunes of War

Once Europe had dominated American cinema, but even World War I was to work in Hollywood's favour. With the European film industries destabilized between 1914 and 1918, the US companies could take a firmer hold on their own industry and also expand more into Europe and other foreign markets. By the end of the war, American films made up 80 per cent of movies being shown on European and other foreign screens, while film-making had become the United States' fifth largest industry.

By 1919, Hollywood was the heart of American film-making and the first movie stars had emerged. 'It is fatal for a producer to sacrifice the production as a whole just to include them in the cast', warned one British trade newspaper. In the 1920s, movie stars power would drive up box-office takings, and stars became America's royalty, with their wealth and sense of entitlement allowing them to enjoy excessive lives of sex and drugs. Overdoses and murder would follow. Hollywood scandal had begun.

Below: The cast and crew of *The Squaw Man* at the end of the first day of filming. The film's director, Cecil B. DeMille, is standing in the centre in the light grey suit.

THE SILENT TWENTIES

In the 1920s, star power reached new heights – Charlie Chaplin, Fatty Arbuckle and Gloria Swanson were each earning $1 million a year. Stars married, remarried and enjoyed numerous affairs, built opulent homes and threw wild parties. Some became drug addicts, at times fatally. They lived high, perhaps fearing that the bubble of their enormous success could easily soon burst. For some it certainly did.

◆

'Hollywood's a place where the circus is permanently in town.'

In 1914 English comedian Charlie Chaplin was touring America in a vaudeville act when he was spotted and signed up for movies with Mack Sennett's Keystone Studios. While at Keystone creating his tramp character, the 25-year-old also pursued his interest in girls of barely legal age. Raoul Walsh, then an actor (later a director), remembered arriving at Keystone one morning to find it closed. The gateman explained that six months earlier a pretty 17-year-old girl had played several small parts, but then found

'All I need to make a comedy is a park, a policeman and a pretty girl,' said Charlie Chaplin. Unfortunately, it was Chaplin's taste in pretty girls that was the trouble. Twice he hurried to Mexico to marry pregnant girlfriends who were under age.

herself pregnant. Her mother approached the District Attorney, but Sennett had a friend in the DA's office, who warned the studio: 'If anybody had anything to do with the girl, tell them to get out of town for a few days.'

'And would you believe it, the whole studio took off,' said the gateman.

'Did Chaplin go?' asked Walsh.

The gateman responded quickly: 'Go? He was the first to leave.'

Chaplin got away that time, but he certainly hadn't learnt his lesson. Four years later, he met 16-year-old actress Mildred Harris. When she later announced that she was pregnant, they quickly married – at that time 17 being the age of consent in California. The pregnancy turned out to be a false alarm and within two years they'd separated. Harris cited Chaplin's mental cruelty as grounds for divorce, but there were rumours that she was in a romantic relationship with lesbian actress Alla Nazimova.

Child Brides

Still, undeterred, in November 1924, when he was 35, Chaplin quickly took 16-year-old Lita Grey (originally Lolita MacMurray) across the border to Mexico to get married. She, too, was already pregnant. He'd first met her when she was seven in Kitty's Come-on Inn tearoom, where her mother was a waitress, and had later cast her in *The Kid* (1921) and *The Gold Rush* (1925). When their son, Charles Spencer Chaplin Jr, was born the following May, Chaplin sent Grey and the baby into hiding until late June, when he could make a birth announcement to the Press – nine months, rather than seven months, after their wedding.

Although Chaplin and Grey had a second child, Sydney Earle Chaplin, Grey is barely mentioned in Chaplin's autobiography. Their unhappy marriage left the perfectionist Chaplin spending as long as possible at the studio finishing *The Gold Rush* and his subsequent film, *The Circus* (1928). In late 1926, Grey took their children and left.

Above: Aviation was one of the early stars' first indulgences. In 1919, Chaplin's brother Sydney launched his own airline. Pictured at Chaplin's aerodrome are, right to left, Charlie Chaplin, his first wife Mildred Harris, and actors Mary Pickford, Marjorie Daw and Douglas Fairbanks.

While Mildred Harris had quietly left with $100,000 and some property, Grey's bill of divorce ran to a lengthy 52 pages, including allegations of infidelity, abuse and descriptions of Chaplin's 'abnormal, unnatural, perverted and degenerate sexual desires'. Such content made headline news and pirated copies of the document were quickly circulated. Keen to limit the bad press, Chaplin agreed to a $600,000 settlement, the highest at that time.

Despite some calls for Chaplin's work to be banned, and with the stress blamed for turning his hair prematurely white, the scandal didn't actually seem to hurt Chaplin's popularity at the box office, and he went on to greater success in the 1930s with *City Lights* (1931) and *Modern Times* (1936).

Chaplin quickly took 16-year-old Lita Grey across the border to Mexico to get married. She, too, was already pregnant.

Below: Lita Grey with her children by Chaplin. In acting for a divorce settlement from Chaplin, Grey's lawyers threatened to reveal the names of 'five prominent motion-picture actresses' with whom Chaplin had been intimate during their brief marriage.

Read the Label

Why did Olive Thomas drink poison? Was it suicide? Was it accidental? And what was that 'poison' doing in her hotel suite anyway?

One of the chorus girls in the Ziegfeld Follies, as well as appearing in Ziegfeld's more risqué Midnight Frolic show, Olive Thomas was also a model, being the first of Alberto Vargas's pin-ups. Moving to Hollywood in 1915, she met actor Jack Pickford, Mary Pickford's younger brother. Though they eloped in 1916, she kept their marriage quiet because she wanted to succeed on her own terms, not as the girlfriend of a famous

CHAPLIN'S FAMILY

IN ALL, CHARLIE Chaplin married four times. His third marriage was to Paulette Goddard (below with Chaplin in *Modern Times* – 1936), who, when they married, was 26 to his 47; his fourth was to Oona O'Neill, who was 18 to his 54. Apart from his marriages, Chaplin also had numerous lovers, including the actresses Pola Negri and Louise Brooks. Brooks would later say that he would always apply iodine before having sex, in the hope that it would protect him against syphilis. Chaplin may have had better understanding than others of the effects of syphilis: his mother had performed on the music hall circuit in England before suffering headaches and a mental breakdown. Chaplin sent her to a mental asylum and in 1921 had her brought out to Hollywood, where she was looked after. It is thought likely that her mental ill health may have been the effects of syphilis.

Chaplin also brought his elder half-brother Sydney out to Hollywood, where he worked as an actor and the star's business manager. In 1929, Sydney, back in Britain, was accused of biting off the nipple of actress Molly Wright in a sexual assault. His British studio settled out of court, conceding the truth of Wright's claims. Following the scandal, Sydney's contract in England was curtailed and he moved on.

Above: Olive Thomas, who died aged 25 in 1920, was one of Hollywood's first celebrity deaths. She had accidentally ingested a topical treatment for her husband's chronic syphilis.

Pickford. 'Two innocent-looking children, they were the gayest, wildest brats who ever stirred the stardust on Broadway,' wrote screenwriter Frances Marion. Unfortunately, 'they were much more interested in playing the roulette of life than in concentrating on their careers.'

While husband Pickford was more of a B-movie actor, Olive Thomas was a star, playing the lead in *The Flapper* (1920), among other films. With work keeping them apart, their marriage suffered and in August 1920 they set off for Paris on a second honeymoon. On the night of 5 September, they returned to their room at the Hotel Ritz having had a lot to drink. Pickford went to bed, while Thomas, according to Pickford, 'fussed around' before drinking liquid mercury bichloride, which had been prescribed as a topical treatment for Pickford's chronic syphilis. When she screamed, Pickford said he jumped out of bed and quickly realized his wife's error. Perhaps in a drunken haze, Thomas had thought the bottle contained water or sleeping pills. Pickford rushed Thomas to hospital but she died five days later of kidney failure.

Suicide or Accident?

The rumours spread quickly and Olive Thomas's death became one of the first major Hollywood scandals. Was it suicide in response to Pickford's adultery? Had he infected her with syphilis? Or had he tricked her into taking the poison? Pickford gave an account of the evening of her death to the *Los Angeles Herald-Examiner,* denying that they'd rowed. He described the bottle as labelled 'Poison', calling it a 'toilet solution' when later explaining its chemical contents. The coroner ruled Thomas's death accidental and Pickford returned with the body by ship to New York.

Above: The wedding of Jack Pickford to actress Marilyn Miller in 1922. An alcoholic like her husband, Miller also suffered from sinus infections and died after complications from nasal surgery in 1936. She was 37.

Little Brother

Jack Pickford's life hadn't been without previous scandal. After the US entered World War I, he joined the US Navy, but used his name to become involved in a scheme that allowed young men to pay bribes to avoid military service, as well as reportedly procuring young women for officers. For his involvement, Pickford came close to being dishonourably discharged.

> Pickford became involved in a scheme that allowed men to pay bribes to avoid military service, as well as reportedly procuring young women for officers.

An alcoholic like his father, Pickford was never a star like his sister Mary or his wife Olive Thomas, and squandered what film career he had. Living recklessly and frivolously, he repeatedly borrowed money from Mary. After Olive Thomas, he married twice more, both times to former Ziegfeld girls. He was physically abusive towards his second wife Marilyn Miller, and by 1923, his acting career was on the wane. His drinking and drug-taking took their toll and he died in 1933, aged 36.

Right: Roscoe 'Fatty' Arbuckle was at the height of his fame as a comedy star when his career fell apart in what is perhaps Hollywood's most notorious sex scandal. He was acquitted of the spurious charges but his career, and his spirit, never recovered.

Arbuckle's Weekend Party

Perhaps the most famous Hollywood scandal is that of Roscoe 'Fatty' Arbuckle. One of the most popular early comedy stars, in 1921 Arbuckle signed a contract with Paramount Pictures for $1 million, the highest of its time, but that was also the year of his downfall.

But was he really a sexual predator? Did he rape, sexually assault and fatally injure Virginia Rappe? Or was he the victim of people exploiting his celebrity over a death for which he wasn't responsible?

In September 1921, Roscoe Arbuckle held a party at the St Francis Hotel in San Francisco. Thirty-year-old Virginia Rappe, an actress known to Arbuckle, joined the party and later that night fell ill. The hotel doctor was called, said she was only drunk, and gave her morphine to calm her. Forty-eight hours later she was admitted to hospital and died the following day from peritonitis caused by a ruptured bladder.

Bambina Maude Delmont, who'd attended the party with Rappe, informed the hospital doctor that Arbuckle

PROHIBITION

FOR MOST AMERICANS, the 1920s was legally the decade of Prohibition (1919–33), but for Hollywood that meant not a time of abstinence but of high living. While the Prohibition laws were sluggishly enforced across the country and came down far more harshly on the working classes than the elites, Hollywood was well accustomed to living on its own terms. Press agents were expected to stockpile booze for their clients, and secretaries were honoured if they were asked to handle their boss's alcohol supply. The studios even charmed journalists by laying on trains full of alcohol to bring the Press from the East Coast to Hollywood for junkets. The frequent crossing of state lines made it easier to bypass Prohibition laws without having to bribe the police.

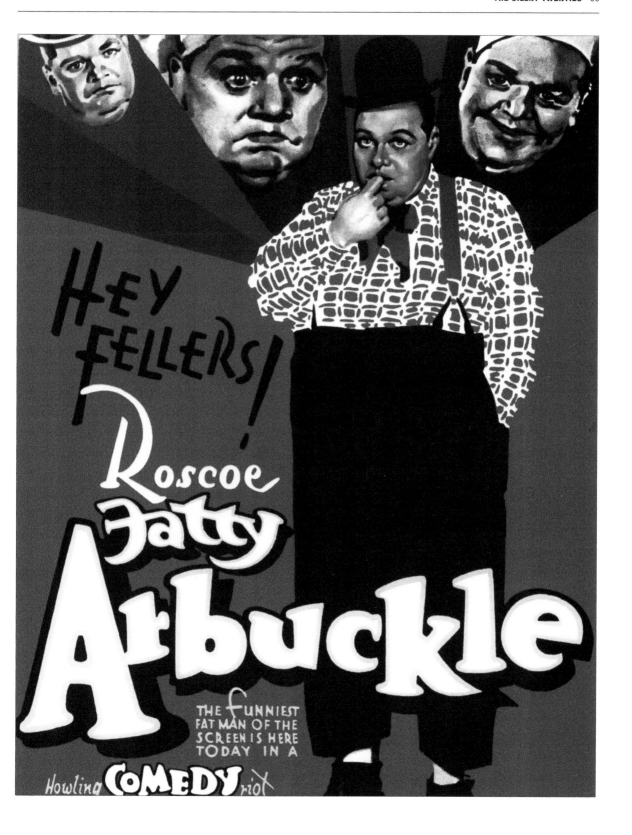

Left: Virginia Rappe died of a ruptured bladder and secondary peritonitis two days after falling ill at Arbuckle's party. 'He hurt me,' a witness had heard Rappe say of Arbuckle, but the actress made no complaint about the star to the doctor who examined her.

had raped her friend. The doctor examined Rappe but found no evidence of rape. When Rappe died, Delmont repeated the rape story to police, who believed it and concluded that Arbuckle's immense weight on Rappe's body had caused the internal injury. Delmont, it should be noted, had previous convictions for extortion, racketeering, fraud and bigamy. It was also alleged that she made a living luring men into compromising positions where they would be photographed as evidence in later divorce proceedings.

At a press conference, Rappe's manager Al Semnacker stated that Arbuckle used a piece of ice to simulate sex with her, which had caused her injuries. By the time this story was reported in the Press, the ice had become a Coca-Cola or champagne bottle. When it came to the trial, witnesses testified that Arbuckle

> Delmont repeated the rape story to police, who believed it and concluded that Arbuckle's immense weight on Rappe's body had caused the internal injury.

had indeed taken a piece of ice, but had merely rubbed it on Rappe's stomach in an attempt to soothe her pain when she'd already fallen ill. However, William Randolph Hearst's newspapers had a field day running speculative stories about the case before and during the trial. Hearst himself later said that the Arbuckle scandal 'sold more newspapers than any event since the

Below: Guilty until proved innocent – this newspaper reports that within days of Virginia Rappe's death – but months before the trial – cinemas across the country had agreed to withdraw Arbuckle's films until he was cleared of manslaughter charges.

MOTION PICTURE DEPARTMENT—PAGES 35 TO 39

Friday, September 16, 1921   **PICTURES**   39

SCANDAL HITS INDUSTRY

TRADE COMMISSION AFTER 'MUSKETEERS'

Gov't Commission Framing Complaint Against 'D'Artagnan' Sponsor

The Federal Trade Commission is framing a complaint against the sponsors of "The Three Musketeers" film now showing at the Manhattan opera house on the ground it unfairly competes with the Douglas Fairbanks feature of the same name at the Lyric. The picture at the Manhattan is controlled by the Triangle Film Corporation, which first produced it in 1916 under the title "D'Artagnan." It is handled by the Film Distributors' League and the Alexander Film Corporation. It is being exhibited for the benefit of the former Rialto theatre orchestra.

The Fairbanks picture is a recent production. O'Brien, Malevinsky & Driscoll, the attorneys, contend the other competes unfairly with their version, although the title itself cannot be copyrighted since the original Dumas work is not thus protected.

"The Triangle's production is advertised as a Thomas H. Ince special, and this has aroused the ire of the director. He has stated that at the time he made the picture he was of no consequence in film circles as a picture director, and that only the past few years he created his "special" trade-mark, and strenuously objects to any such billing in connection with this production.

Arbuckle Affair Furnishes Capital to Screen's Enemies — Hundreds of Exhibitors Cancel "Fatty Comedies"—Some Authorities Ban Subjects for Present —Actor Indicted for Manslaughter—Murder Charge Stands.

San Francisco, Sept. 14.
Roscoe Arbuckle's attorneys are this afternoon making a fight to obtain the release of the film comedian. The grand jury handed down an indictment against Arbuckle of manslaughter in the first degree. It is on this indictment his attorneys want him freed on bail. In the police court the charge of murder still stands against him and District Attorney Matthew Brady is fighting his admission to bail on the ground that the police court hearing will first have to be heard.

Since his arrival here Saturday Arbuckle has been lodged in jail without bail. His attorneys and Lou Anger, Joseph M. Schenck's representative in Los Angeles, have been the only ones permitted to see him at his own request. His arrest was made on the murder charge following the death of Virginia Rappe in a private sanitarium last Friday, following her breakdown in the rooms of the comedian at the St. Francis Hotel the previous Monday during a "wild party."

The district attorney is trying to locate between 20 and 30 people present in the comedian's rooms Monday at various times during the course of the party. He is also charging witnesses have been intimidated and intimates that a number of arrests will follow on the ground that perjury has been committed by some of the wit-

mer still remains fresh in public memory.
At the Tuesday meeting of the Theatre Owners Chamber of Commerce of Greater New York a resolution was passed to withdraw all Arbuckle pictures from exhibition in over 600 houses in the greater city until such time that the comedian should be cleared of the charge of murder. There were demonstrations at a number of houses where greater announcing the appearance of Arbuckle was posted. In one house all the paper was mutilated and in another boohs and hisses greeted slides of the comedian.

From all points in the country reports have been issued by exhibitors that they are withdrawing the "Fatty" pictures.

In most instances the exhibitors have acted on their own initiative and stopped the films but in other localities the authorities have issued orders for the police to prohibit the showing of the pictures.

The New York State Board of Censors announced that the state law does not permit interference with the exhibition of films under such circumstances or because of any personal act of any person appearing in a picture or pictures.

Arbuckle is under contract to Famous Players for three years, at a salary of $3,500 a week and 25 per cent of the profits on his pictures, the profits being divided between him

Department of Public Safety to prohibit the showing of Arbuckle films in this city.

Pittsburgh, Sept. 14.
A meeting of the Pennsylvania Association of M. P. Owners has placed the ban on the showing of Arbuckle films in their houses in this State until he has been cleared of the crime charged to him in San Francisco.

The mayors of Cambridge, Lynn, Everett and Medford have prohibited the showing of any Arbuckle films in those cities because of the sordid circumstances surrounding the arrest of the comedian.

Providence, Sept. 14.
The Providence Police Commission has ordered the withdrawal of all Arbuckle films from the local screens.

Memphis, Sept. 14.
The Memphis Board of Censors stated yesterday no showings of Arbuckle pictures would be permitted in the city until he had cleared himself of the murder charge.

Chicago, Sept. 14.
Jones, Linick & Schaeffer, the Ascher Brothers and Lubliner & Trinz have barred the Arbuckle pictures from their houses until the comedian is cleared of the charges against him.

FILM STARS' STUNT CAUSES BOSTON RIOT

Police Called Out to Clear For Traffic When Fairbanks-Pickford Arrive

Boston, Sept. 14.
The Pickford-Fairbanks publicity stunt for "The Three Musketeers" at the Selwyn this week got away from them entirely, and developed into a genuine riot, with police reserves called out, streets patroled and free fights in the Hotel Touraine.

The Boston Post, which claims the largest morning circulation in America, sponsored the publicity stunt, "leading" the paper with it for two days and conducting an automobile tour by published route for the two stars and Mrs. Pickford over the road from New York, leading up to the premiere at a $1.50 top at the Selwyn, which never in its history has shown pictures before.

The house was sold out three days before the opening of the picture, and a Sunday matinee and a Monday matinee were then announced, these both selling out immediately at the same price scale. Saturday, Sunday and Monday the streets were so badly blocked police reserves had to be called out for hours at a time to permit traffic to pass. During one mad rush Monday into the Hotel Touraine, a porter was shoved into the elevator well and so badly injured that he had to be removed to the hospital.

The two stars confined their appearance in the theatre to a few words from a box. Coming over the road from New York the stars his

Above: Arbuckle was supported in court by his wife Minta Durfree who maintained that he was the 'nicest man in the world,' even though they'd privately and amicably separated well before the scandal.

> Arbuckle had many fans in the public gallery, but also enemies outside – his wife was shot at as she entered the courthouse one day.

sinking of the RMS *Lusitania*'. At first, the judge found no evidence of rape and dismissed that charge, but, on the strength of Zey Prevon, a party witness, who stated that Rappe had said 'He hurt me' regarding Arbuckle, he then allowed a murder charge to proceed, although it was later reduced to manslaughter.

The trial began in November 1921 with Arbuckle supported by his estranged wife, Minta Durfree. Arbuckle had many fans in the public gallery, but

also enemies outside – Durfree even being shot at one day while entering the courthouse. In court, the prosecution's evidence soon began to fall apart, with Betty Campbell, a party guest, admitting that San Francisco's District Attorney, Matthew Brady, had threatened to charge her with perjury if she didn't testify against Arbuckle. Dr Edward Heinrich, a local criminologist, had claimed to have found Arbuckle's fingerprints in Rappe's bloodstains on the hotel suite's bathroom door, but this was disproven when it was revealed that the room had been cleaned before Heinrich had examined it and no blood remained. Dr Beardsee, the hotel doctor who'd first examined

Virginia Rappe, said that it appeared an external force seemed to have damaged her bladder, but admitted that when he examined her she hadn't mentioned being assaulted. Pathologists, however, stated that there didn't seem to be any external cause for the rupture. Rather, it was noted in court that Rappe had had existing health problems, including chronic cystitis. Arbuckle took the stand and explained that after he'd found Rappe vomiting in his room during the party, he and other guests had tried to help her. After a two-week trial, the jury returned deadlocked with a 10–2 not guilty verdict and a mistrial was declared.

At the second trial two months later, the defence was permitted to reveal details about Rappe's character, including her promiscuity and her heavy drinking, which inflamed her chronic cystitis. Another witness, who'd claimed he'd been bribed not to testify about Arbuckle raping Rappe, turned out to be a criminal who was in collusion with the DA in an effort to reduce his own sentence. With his team confident of an acquittal, Arbuckle didn't take the stand, but some of the jurors interpreted this as an indication of guilt. Again the jury was deadlocked, but this time with a 9–3 verdict to convict. A second mistrial was declared.

A Six-Minute Verdict

At the third trial in March 1922, the defence was taking no chances. While Arbuckle testified, his attorney attacked Rappe's character and in his closing statement described Bambina Maude Delmont as 'the complaining witness who never witnessed'. Equally, as Zey Prevon was now out of the country, the prosecution lost their witness who had heard Rappe's 'He hurt me' line. While the first two juries had spent 44 hours and 40 hours respectively deliberating over their verdict, the third jury returned within six minutes. They found Arbuckle not guilty. In addition, they offered a statement of apology to Arbuckle. 'Acquittal is not enough for Roscoe Arbuckle,' they told the court. 'We feel that a great injustice has been done to him... there was not the slightest proof adduced to connect him in any way with the commission of a crime. He was manly throughout the case and told a straightforward story which we all believe. We wish him success and hope that the American people will take the judgement of twelve men and women that Roscoe Arbuckle is entirely innocent and free from all blame.'

Their wish wasn't granted: Arbuckle was already ruined. Although he left the court with only the $500 fine to pay for breaking the Prohibition laws, six days later he found himself formally shut out of Hollywood. Even before the trial, the studios had ordered their stars not to stand by Arbuckle, with Buster Keaton, who worked independently, a lone voice in making a statement in support of Arbuckle's innocence. And even before the verdict, the studios had banned his films being screened. No matter what the jury thought, the Press and court hearings had revealed that he'd broken the Prohibition laws and was throwing parties with actresses. This gave the lie to the studio's image of him as a happy family man (although he and Durfree had already amicably and privately separated). In

> Although the ban on Arbuckle working was lifted after six months, the studios had already washed their hands of him.

Hollywood, you could get up to all kinds of things that the studios knew about, as long as the general public didn't find out. Although the ban on Arbuckle working was lifted after six months, the studios had already washed their hands of him. Or perhaps they judged that the public had turned away from him. Either way, a man who'd signed a million-dollar contract a year earlier now couldn't get a job.

Even before the third trial, Bambina Maude Delmont had been touring the country with a one-woman show called 'The woman who signed the murder charge against Arbuckle' and lecturing on the evils of Hollywood. This tour would have made her some money, but had she hoped to extort money from Arbuckle with a rape claim that had escalated beyond her control?

Arbuckle had to sell his house and his cars to pay legal fees in excess of $700,000. Buster Keaton found him some writing and directing work, but Arbuckle fell into alcoholism. 'Roscoe only seemed to find solace and comfort in a bottle,' said Durfree, who'd now divorced him, but always maintained that he was the nicest man in the world and that they were still friends.

In the later 1920s and early 1930s, Arbuckle began directing under the pseudonym William Goodrich. But his heart wasn't in it. 'He made no attempt to direct this picture,' said Louise Brooks, who appeared in one of these films. 'He sat in his chair like a man dead. He had been very nice and sweetly dead ever since the scandal that ruined his career.'

In 1932, Arbuckle signed a contract with Warner Bros. to appear in six short films under his own name again. They were successful, but he died the following year of heart failure, aged 46. It seems likely that Arbuckle was an innocent man whose career was ruined by a corrupt DA, by Bambina Maude Delmont's attempt to extort money from him, by a Press willing to print unfounded scandal, and by a scared film industry that treated him like a gangrenous limb. It couldn't allow itself to be infected any more.

Reel Trouble

Even before the third Arbuckle trial had taken place, another huge scandal had rocked Tinseltown. One morning in February 1922, the houseboy of director William Desmond Taylor arrived at Taylor's LA home

> Despite the gunshot wound, a doctor examined the body and declared that the director had died of a ruptured stomach ulcer.

to find his employer dead. A doctor soon appeared on the scene, examined the body and declared that the director had died of a ruptured stomach ulcer. So it was odd then that when people turned Taylor's body over, it was revealed that he'd been shot in the back. Perhaps not so odd was that the doctor was never identified and never seen again. If he wasn't a complete fraud, he certainly wouldn't want to own up to such incompetence.

Right: Buster Keaton with his wife Natalie Talmadge in *Our Hospitality*. Keaton's own hospitality extended to bringing one of his lovers home and inviting her to choose from his wife's extensive wardrobe.

BUSTER KEATON

THROUGHOUT THE 1920S, Buster Keaton enjoyed his greatest run of success making his films independently and with no studio interference. So what went wrong? In simple terms, a mixture of professional and personal disaster. Keaton's run of hits stumbled with *The General* (1927). Although it's now regarded as his greatest film, audiences were uncomfortable with a comic story set against the American Civil War. Ambitious to make, the film was a misfire at the box office and United Artists, who distributed Keaton's movies, demanded greater supervision over his budgets. Two films later, Keaton, never a businessman, gave up his independence and went to work under contract at MGM. He'd lost the artistic freedom he'd had in the 1920s and would never be as successful again. Although he kept working solidly for the rest of his life, his peak had passed with the arrival of the talkies.

But his private life was difficult, too. A womanizer before he'd married, his wife, actress Natalie Talmadge, sister-in-law of his boss, Joseph Schenck, was a virgin

on their wedding night. While they had courted briefly some time earlier, they hadn't seen each other for two years when she wrote to Keaton: 'If you still care for me, just send for me.' Keaton went East to see her and they married. After the birth of their second child in 1924, however, Talmadge announced that she was no longer interested in sex and turned him out of their bedroom. Keaton replied that in that case he'd take other lovers, which he did.

He also became more of a drinker, his marriage finally collapsing after Keaton invited one of his mistresses to their home, telling her to help herself to his wife's huge wardrobe – it being alleged that Talmadge spent a third of their money on clothes. Talmadge finally divorced Keaton in 1932, taking much of his fortune and refusing to allow any contact between Keaton and his sons for a decade. With the failure of his marriage, and the loss of his independence as a film-maker, by the mid-1930s Keaton had gone bust and was a hopeless alcoholic.

Witzel

Sincerely.
Mabel Normand

Left: Although Mabel Normand was ruled out as a suspect in William Desmond Taylor's death, because she had visited him the evening before he died and was the last person to admit seeing him alive, her career was damaged by association.

> When the police arrived, Mabel Normand was searching for her love letters to the director and Paramount executives were busy burning documents.

controlling mother Charlotte Shelby? Or by Sands, his valet, who'd fled two weeks earlier, having stolen from Taylor? (But who might also have been Taylor's brother who'd disappeared a decade earlier.) With that cast of suspects, perhaps soap operas don't have such outlandish plots after all.

Word spread quickly around Hollywood about the 49-year-old director's death. By the time the police arrived, quite a crowd of Hollywood insiders was already at the scene. As Minter was screaming out her love for Taylor, a package of her love letters was being found in the toe of one of Taylor's riding boots and a pink satin nightgown monogramed with 'MMM' in his wardrobe, Mabel Normand was searching for *her* old love letters to the director, and Paramount executives were busy burning documents. The alleged pornographic photos in which Taylor appeared with well-known actresses were never found.

So, who shot William Desmond Taylor? Was it his friend actress Mabel Normand – a frequent co-star of Roscoe Arbuckle's – who'd visited him the night he died? Or was he murdered by teenage star Mary Miles Minter, who was in love with him? Or by Minter's

But who was William Desmond Taylor? Not, it seemed, William Desmond Taylor. He was, in fact, William Cunningham Deane-Tanner from Ireland, married with a daughter and working as an antique dealer in New York when, in 1908, following an affair with a married woman, he'd disappeared. A brother, Denis Deane-Tanner, had followed Taylor to New York but was continually borrowing money from him. Four years after Taylor disappeared, Denis did, too.

Left: Mary Miles Minter and her director William Desmond Taylor. After Taylor was found shot dead, Minter became one of the suspects. She'd been infatuated with him and a pink satin nightgown monogrammed with the letters 'MMM' was discovered at his home.

Above: Mary Miles Minter in 1937 when her sister, Margaret Fillmore, sued their mother Charlotte Shelby over a family financial dispute. In the court hearings, the William Desmond Taylor case came up again, with Fillmore saying her mother: 'would kill anybody for $1000.'

As Taylor's missing years were pieced together, it was learnt that he'd been to Alaska prospecting for gold, had worked as a bookkeeper in a mine and as a stockbroker in Chicago, among many other jobs, before winding up in Hollywood as an actor in 1912. There he moved from acting to becoming a successful director. Hollywood – always a great place for reinvention.

And what of the suspects? After fleeing, Taylor's valet Sands had sent Taylor a pawn stub bearing the name 'William Deane-Tanner', indicating that he knew Taylor's true identity. Had he reappeared to blackmail Taylor and in the altercation shot him? Sands was never found. If he wasn't Taylor's brother, that makes two people from the director's life who disappeared.

Could the murder have been related to drugs? Eighteen months earlier, Taylor had appealed to an assistant US attorney for help in breaking up the traffic

DRUG ADDICTS

FOR AS LONG as the Hollywood film industry has existed, there have always been drug casualties. When action hero Wallace Reid was injured in a stunt in 1919, he was prescribed morphine to numb the pain so that he could carry on filming. However, he became addicted to them and he eventually had to be sent to a sanatorium. It was already too late and, in 1923, at the age of 31, he died locked in a padded cell. After his death, his widow, actress and director Dorothy Davenport, called for greater awareness of drug addiction.

Barbara La Marr (pictured below with Douglas Fairbanks in *The Three Musketeers* – 1921) was a burlesque dancer, a sometime call girl, a successful screenwriter and an actress. When, in 1924, she was found unconscious, her studio, MGM, had her committed to a sanatorium. However, the following year she was arrested carrying 40 cubes of morphine. She was too weak to stand trial for her offence and died in January 1926. The coroner was persuaded by MGM to attribute her death to tuberculosis, but she'd actually died of a cocaine overdose.

Married briefly to studio executive Dr Daniel Carson Goodman, actress Alma Rubens's drug was morphine, after it was prescribed when she was suffering from a 'minor ailment'. Quickly becoming addicted, she later admitted she began to take morphine for every real and imagined illness. In 1926 and then again in 1929, she was too ill to continue working.

Ruben's addiction was kept from the public until 1929, when she attempted to stab a physician who was taking her to a sanatorium. Although being held under guard, she later managed to escape hospital, clean up and went back to work, before being arrested on a drugs charge in San Diego in 1931. She claimed that it was a frame-up and physicians backed her up: she wasn't taking drugs. Shortly after her release, though, she contracted pneumonia and died quickly, aged 33.

in drugs, mentioning that a well-known actress friend was being extorted by peddlers for $2000 a month. The actress was Mabel Normand; the drug was cocaine. Some suggest that a hit was put on Taylor because he was trying to expose the cocaine dealers.

Or could the killer have been Mary Miles Minter's jealous mother, Charlotte Shelby? Actress Colleen Moore, a contemporary of Minter's, described Shelby as 'one of those well-born Southern women who never let anyone, including the fan-magazines, forget it'. Shelby had managed a lucrative Hollywood deal for her child star daughter, with herself as guardian.

LOUISE BROOKS

LOUISE BROOKS, ONE of the most distinctive faces of the silent era, didn't want to play the Hollywood game, and at the height of her fame in the late 1920s she left Hollywood to work, admittedly also very successfully, in Germany. When she returned, sound had come in and she'd lost her footing, and when offered the female lead in *The Public Enemy* (1931), she turned it down to pursue a love affair in New York.

Seeming to lack the ruthless ambition necessary to maintain star status, her career faded during the 1930s and she briefly headed back to her hometown of Wichita. 'But that turned out to be another kind of hell,' she would later admit. 'The citizens of Wichita either resented me having been a success or despised me for being a failure.'

Some time later she even worked for a few years as a salesgirl in Saks Fifth Avenue in New York City and admitted to having been a courtesan to a few clients in the early 1940s: 'I found that the only well-paying career open to me, as an unsuccessful actress of thirty-six, was that of a call girl … and [I] began to flirt with the fancies related to little bottles filled with yellow sleeping pills.'

A heavy drinker from childhood, she was sexually liberated and had many lovers, including a one-night stand with Greta Garbo. However, of women she said: 'Out of curiosity, I had two affairs with girls – they did nothing for me.'

> He'd told Minter that she was too young for him, besides which he was in love with Mabel Normand.

But Minter was 18 now. 'The thought of losing this gold-mine daughter to a husband filled Mama with such terror she became almost insanely jealous,' wrote Moore. Neighbour Faith MacLean testified at a preliminary hearing that she'd heard a gunshot the previous evening at the house and she had seen someone who looked like a woman dressed as a man leave the property. Could it have been Charlotte Shelby, who didn't want a relationship between Minter and Taylor to cut her out of a Hollywood fortune? If that was her thinking, it seems misjudged, because Minter's love for Taylor was unrequited – although he had kept her love letters. He'd told Minter that she was too young for him, besides which he was in love with Mabel Normand.

Ultimately, no one was ever charged with Taylor's murder. It remains a fascinating whodunit with no conclusion. The case, however, still had its casualties. Minter's letters to Taylor, which had actually been written three years earlier, found their way into the newspapers, and, combined with the story that there might have been some relationship between the teenager and the middle-aged man, did a great deal to tarnish her demure image. Her films were withdrawn from distribution and the following year Paramount passed on the opportunity to renew her contract. She turned down other offers and, at the age of 21, retired from acting. Two years later she sued her mother for the money she had received during Minter's career. They settled out of court. For her part, Mabel Normand's career continued, but her tuberculosis reoccurred the following year and she died in 1930, at the age of 37.

The murder of William Desmond Taylor has all the makings of a Hollywood movie, but it might have to be a comedy to be taken seriously.

Right: Louise Brooks was free-spirited both on and off screen. 'We were all marvellously degenerate and happy,' she said of Hollywood in the 1920s. 'We were a world of our own and outsiders didn't intrude.'

The Power of the Press

In November 1924, one single morning edition of *The Los Angeles Times* ran the headline: *'Movie Producer Shot on Hearst Yacht!'* 'Hearst' was William Randolph Hearst, the immensely powerful newspaper and film baron, and the 'movie producer' was Thomas Ince, who'd been working in Hollywood for 20 years and owned his own studio. Given such a story, it was surprising it didn't reappear or develop in the evening edition or any subsequent editions of that paper or other newspapers. But it didn't. Nor was the story corrected as might be expected if the shooting report had been an error. Later reports of Ince's death simply stated that after suffering from stomach ulcers, he'd had a fatal heart attack at home. No mention of a shooting was made, and, two days later, his body was cremated.

> Ince's death simply stated that after suffering from stomach ulcers, he'd had a fatal heart attack at home. No mention of a shooting was made, and, two days later, his body was cremated.

According to other Hearst newspapers, Ince had first fallen ill while visiting the Hearst California ranch, San Simeon, and had been rushed home by ambulance, where he'd died surrounded by his family. But it was the shooting headline that captured the popular imagination. There are various versions of the story; all point the finger at Hearst. As D.W. Griffith said: 'All you have to do to make Hearst turn white as a ghost is mention Ince's name. There's plenty wrong there, but Hearst is too big.'

The story goes that Hearst suspected that his long-time lover Marion Davies was having an affair with Charlie Chaplin. To find out if this was true, Hearst invited Chaplin to join them at a party on his yacht *Oneida* off the Californian coast. Among others present were journalist Louella Parsons, author Elinor Glyn and Dr Daniel Carson Goodman, a non-practising physician who worked as a studio executive and was married to star Alma Rubens, who wasn't on board. One night, Hearst found Chaplin and Davies talking, and, enraged by jealousy, pulled out a gun. Davies's screams alerted Ince, who came running, and, in the scuffle over Hearst's gun, was shot. Another version had Hearst seeing Ince talking to Davies in the darkness, and, mistaking him for Chaplin, shot him. Or was Ince caught by a ricocheting bullet? Or perhaps Ince was in bed with Davies.

The rumours about Ince's death were strong enough for the San Diego District Attorney to open an investigation. Dr Goodman testified that Ince had fallen ill and that he'd brought him ashore. While taking the train back to Los Angeles, Ince's condition was so bad that they left the train early and were seen by a physician. Finally making it home, Ince died just over two days after the party.

Until then, Louella Parsons had been a film columnist for Hearst's newspaper *The New York American*. But after Ince's death, Hearst gave her a lifetime contract and moved her to *The Los Angeles Examiner*, putting her at the heart of Hollywood and syndicating her columns widely. She became one of Hollywood's leading gossip columnists. Had Hearst simply recognized a good talent or was he buying her silence on the Ince matter?

And what of the anomalies? Why the *'Movie Producer Shot on Hearst Yacht!'* headline if there was no substance to it? Someone must have put the newspaper on to the scent of the story, even if it was wrong. Why did a Hearst newspaper later print that Ince had been taken ill at a party at the Hearst ranch, not on the yacht? Although both Chaplin and Louella Parsons claimed that they'd not even been on the yacht and Parsons had said she'd been in New York at the time, others said that they'd seen her in Hollywood with Davies just before leaving to board the *Oneida*. If the case was considered important enough for the San Diego DA to investigate, why did he then call on only one witness, Dr Goodman, to testify? Also, Chaplin's driver Toraichi Kono claimed that he had seen Ince reach the shore and it looked as if his head was 'bleeding from a bullet wound'. Like the death of William Desmond Taylor, Thomas Ince's has prompted a great deal of speculation that will never now be solved.

Right: Gossip columnist Louella Parsons (centre) leaving Hearst offices. Despite rumours, she denied being on Hearst's yacht the weekend that Thomas Ince fell ill. But soon after Ince's death she was promoted by Hearst, leading to suggestions that Hearst had bought her silence.

> Hays banned Arbuckle from working in Hollywood and had Mary Miles Minter's films pulled from distribution.

The Hays Office

After the Chaplin weddings and public divorces, and the Arbuckle and Taylor scandals, the film industry needed to clean up shop. So William H. Hays, a former postmaster-general in President Harding's administration, was hired as the first president of the Motion Pictures Producers and Distributors of America (MPPDA).

The MPPDA, which represented the studio heads and became better known as the Hays Office, introduced morality clauses into stars' contracts, enabling the studios to fire or fine them if they were involved in a scandal. It was Hays who banned Arbuckle from working in Hollywood, and Hays who had Mary Miles Minter's films pulled from circulation after the Taylor murder. The Hays Office would go on to have immense influence in vetting scripts on matters of decency and censoring films.

Right: Gloria Swanson and Walter Byron in *Queen Kelly*. **One of the biggest stars of the silent era, Swanson is now actually best known for her role in 1950's** *Sunset Boulevard*, **in which she played a former silent movie star.**

The Coming of Sound

By the end of the 1920s, the stars were playing the studios off against each other and increasing their fees. In an effort to claw back some control and reduce the competition, some studios, such as First National and Paramount, merged to give themselves more clout.

But star status was also about to be challenged by the coming of sound. When the idea of producing talking pictures was first proposed, Harry Warner said: 'Who the hell wants to hear actors talk?' For him, the bonus of sound was in watching and hearing orchestras play. Nevertheless, his studio went ahead and produced *The Jazz Singer* (1927), the first

JOSEPH P. KENNEDY SNR

JOSEPH KENNEDY, PRESIDENT
John F. Kennedy's father, was a
hugely successful businessman and
stockbroker in the 1920s. In 1923
he expanded into buying cinemas
and was interested, like the moguls,
in making the move into producing
films as well. Contrary to rumours,
there is no evidence that he was a
bootlegger, but womanizing and
sharp practice weren't beyond
him. In 1926, with his wife Rose
(pictured with Kennedy) at home
in Massachusetts with their first
seven children, Kennedy moved
to Hollywood.

There he began an affair with
Gloria Swanson, the biggest star
of the time. She was married to
French aristocrat Henri, Marquis
de la Falaise de la Coudraye, but
Kennedy gave the Marquis a job
at Pathé (USA), which required
him to represent the company in
Paris for ten months of the year.
Conveniently, the Marquis was
now out of the way. Kennedy and
Swanson's relationship was an
open secret in Hollywood and he
also became her business partner,
organizing the financing for her
next few films and producing her
movie *Queen Kelly* (1929). When,
though, after three years, the affair
with Kennedy ended, Swanson
found herself worse off than before.
'Joe Kennedy operated just like
Joe Stalin,' she wrote years later.
'Their system was to write a letter
to the files and then order the exact
reverse on the phone.' She was left
a million and a half dollars in debt.

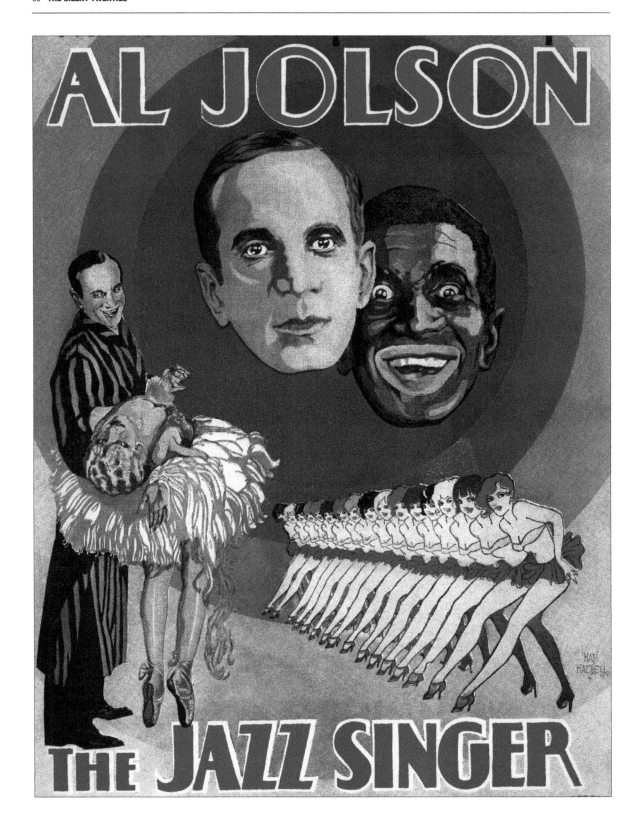

Above: Will Hays (standing second from right at the door), President of the Motion Pictures Producers and Distributors of America (MPPDA), showing how his film censorship office worked.

> Mary Pickford's acid comment was that 'adding sound to movies would be like putting lipstick on the Venus de Milo'.

talkie. After the first screening, the audience of movie insiders filed out of the auditorium in silence. 'They were terrified,' said Frances Goldwyn, Sam Goldwyn's

Left: *The Jazz Singer* (1927) was the first talkie. 'The coming of sound,' said Louise Brooks, 'meant the end of Hollywood's all-night parties. You had to rush back from the studios and start learning your lines, ready for the next day's shooting.'

second wife, while Mary Pickford's acid comment was that 'adding sound to movies would be like putting lipstick on the Venus de Milo'. Pickford did make some sound films, but her career faded with the talkies, perhaps also because in the cruelty of Hollywood cinema, there were, and still are, fewer roles for women over the age of 35. She retired from acting in 1933, at the age of 41, but remained a producer. Not all actors had the voices or the style that would transfer to talking pictures, however. The careers of Buddy Rogers, Colleen Moore and Norma Talmadge all waned with the era of sound.

THE OSCARS

THE OSCARS MIGHT seem to have been created to celebrate Hollywood's best work, but were, in fact, a by-product of an effort to pre-empt the growing interest in organized labour in Tinseltown. By setting up, in 1927, the Academy of Motion Picture Arts and Sciences, Louis B. Mayer was really attempting to keep Hollywood players on side. 'Who needs a union, when you have the fellowship of the Academy?' went the reasoning.

And while Mayer hadn't been part of the Will Hays-led MPPDA effort to control Hollywood's morals on and off screen, he was chairman of the Academy. At first the Academy only held an annual banquet, at which 231 people signed up for $100 annual membership, but in 1929 the first Academy Awards were added to the dinner. Hollywood, Mayer had recognized, could earn some respectability for its movies by awarding itself prizes.

Quite why the statuette has become known as an Oscar, no one is sure. Bette Davis claimed that she named it after her first husband, band leader Harmon Oscar Nelson. Another claim is that the Academy's executive secretary, Margaret Herrick, said the statuette reminded her of her 'Uncle Oscar' – her nickname, in fact, for her cousin Oscar Pierce. And after journalist Sidney Skolsky picked up on this and repeated it in his column, 'Employees have affectionately dubbed their famous statuette "Oscar",' the name stuck.

Above: Douglas Fairbanks presents Janet Gaynor with her Best Actress Oscar at the first Academy Awards in 1929.

Karl Dane, a silent comedy star, had had the luxury houses and Rolls-Royces, but he spoke with a strong Danish accent. With the coming of sound, his career faltered and he was dropped by MGM. He tried a mining business venture, which failed, and working as a mechanic and waiter, but lost his jobs, and by 1934 he was selling hotdogs outside Paramount Studios. Soon after that, he shot himself. His body would have gone unclaimed if Buster Keaton and Danish actor Jean Hersholt hadn't appealed to MGM's management, who liked to present the company as one big family, and shamed the studio into paying for a funeral.

There may have been some dirty tricks, too. It's been alleged that Louis B. Mayer's dislike for star John Gilbert was so intense he intentionally had Gilbert's voice recorded without any bass so that it came out sounding squeaky, making the audience laugh. Whatever the truth, it's certainly the case that Gilbert's career stalled in the 1930s, his contract with MGM wasn't renewed and in 1936 he died of alcoholism.

> Once a star with luxury houses and Rolls-Royces, by 1934 Karl Dane was selling hotdogs outside Paramount Studios.

By the late 1920s, star power had been checked, the coming of sound had ended some careers, and lives, and the studios had reasserted themselves. New codes of morality on and off screen had been introduced and would be enforced, tested and twisted. For the next 20 years the stars' lives would, for better and for worse, be under the control of the studio system.

Below: Karl Dane (left) and John Gilbert in 1925's *The Big Parade*. Both of their careers failed with the coming of sound. Dane committed suicide in 1934, while Gilbert was an alcoholic and died from a heart attack in 1936.

III

THE STUDIO SYSTEM

The coming of sound had ruined some actors' careers and the Depression had sent many studios into the red, but the 1930s and 1940s would see Hollywood grow into its most powerful form ever. Yet the success of the golden age was achieved through a controlling hold over movie stars and was maintained by the collusion of the Los Angeles police force and the district attorney, as well as the Press, in covering up sex scandals and possibly murder.

◆

'They taught me how to be a star, but not how to live.'

Each studio – MGM, Paramount, Warner Brothers, Fox, RKO, Universal and Columbia being the majors – was, by the 1930s, like a miniature city, with its staff of actors, writers, producers, directors, designers, cinematographers, composers, editors, sound technicians and carpenters, as well as barbers, dentists, schools and fire brigades. MGM, the richest studio with 4000 people on the payroll, even had its own branch line railway.

The Dream Factory – Warner Bros. studios in Burbank, California, during the 1940s, when it was producing 40 films a year, including *Casablanca*. Not just stars, but writers, producers, directors and all the necessary crew worked under long contracts at most studios.

Being signed up to a major studio was what all movie actors sought, but to achieve that they would have to give away a great deal in return. Firstly, actors signed seven-year contracts. Why seven years? Because that was the longest Californian law would allow. But, while the studio could review the contract every six months and release an actor, the actor didn't enjoy the same get-out rights. And though the pay for stars could be wonderful, the bigger names earning a few thousand dollars a week, starting salaries began at $50. Even then, contracts were for only 40 weeks a year, with the other 12 weeks an unpaid 'vacation' period, during which actors weren't allowed to work elsewhere. 'So, instead of getting $50 a week for the first year, it worked out at $35,' said Ava Gardner, who arrived as a 17-year-old starlet in 1941. 'Out of that you always had to be well-groomed and shell out for your food and a place to live.' But what would some of the young, pretty

Selznick International PRESENTS

Rebecca
starring
LAURENCE OLIVIER · JOAN FONTAINE
hero of "Wuthering Heights"   *in her sensational starring debut*
GEORGE SANDERS · JUDITH ANDERSON
Directed by ALFRED HITCHCOCK · *From the best selling novel by* DAPHNE DU MAURIER
Produced by DAVID O. SELZNICK *who made "Gone With the Wind" · Released thru* UNITED ARTISTS

Above: In the studio system, if actors under contract turned down scripts, they could be suspended and the period of suspension added to their contract. Joan Fontaine's seven-year contract with David O. Selznick, who produced *Rebecca*, eventually lasted a decade.

actresses do if they were hard up and weren't allowed to take on other official work? 'Many of the starlets and contract players had to put out,' said Ava Gardner. 'Plenty of them thought nothing of giving a little bit away when the rental was due.'

While many starlets were let go after six months, for other players a seven-year contract could easily last much longer. 'If the studio didn't have a script ready for you,' said Joan Fontaine, who starred in *Rebecca*, 'they would send you one that they knew you would turn down.' That way, as she was technically suspended, they didn't have to pay her until they had something

> 'Many of the starlets had to put out,' said Ava Gardner. 'Plenty of them thought nothing of giving a bit away when the rental was due.'

suitable. 'It was a terrible tyranny because the actor had to capitulate,' she said. In addition, the length of the suspension wouldn't count as part of her time under contract. Due to such suspensions, Fontaine's seven-year contract with studio head David O. Selznick ended up lasting a decade.

And, even if an actor managed to get himself fired in order to be released from a contract, the other studios wouldn't snap him up – word probably already having

SUICIDE AT THE HOLLYWOOD SIGN

ERECTED IN 1923 as 'Hollywoodland' to advertise housing developments, the Hollywood sign was only intended to last 18 months, but as 'Hollywood' became more than just a locality and the international label for American movies, the sign was kept up. Nine years later, 24-year-old Peg Entwistle climbed up the workman's ladder to the top of the 'H' of the Hollywoodland sign and threw herself off. She'd been a successful stage actress on Broadway, and, during the Depression, had moved to Hollywood. But she'd only appeared in one film and hadn't been signed up by a studio. As the movies hadn't given her a new life, the Hollywood sign would be the means of her death.

circulated that he was trouble. One might wonder why actors agreed to such unfavourable terms, but they were grateful for the work. That was just the way things were under the studio system.

Those who became stars didn't just owe their careers to the studios, they usually even owed them money. Expected to be seen living the high life, the studios set their stars up with grand houses and domestic staff, and when the stars became stretched financially, the studios would then lend them money. It was a good way for the studios to keep their stars dependent and therefore loyal.

At MGM the involvement of the studio in the private lives of its stars even extended to a chart in the main production office following each actress's menstrual cycle. That way the studio could schedule filming around days when she might not be at her best. Actors and actresses were also subject to their contracts' 'potato clause', which stipulated that their weight must be kept within a certain range. According to Irene Mayer, Louis B. Mayer's daughter, actresses with a weight problem might even be given worms to help them lose some pounds.

Damage Limitation

'If you get into trouble,' MGM's stars were told, 'Don't call the police. Don't call the hospital. Don't call your lawyer. Call Howard.' Howard was Howard Strickling, the studio's head of publicity. Yes, his office would provide benign press releases about the studio's stars, but he would also orchestrate cover-ups when his stars were in danger of making the headlines through brawls, sex scandals and even shootings.

To achieve near silence when it was needed, Strickling and the other studios had friends in the police. The studios created a great deal of wealth for Los Angeles, so it was in the city's interest to keep Hollywood in a good light. Heads of police and local politicians were frequent visitors at the studios – not because they were investigating crimes or discussing employment law, but because they were having their photographs taken with stars and promoting themselves

Below: Buron Fitts (left) with his wife and friends at a première in 1930, was the Los Angeles County District Attorney who, according to Budd Schulberg, 'was completely in the pocket of the producers.'

Right: If the rumour went round that a star was gay, his studio might set up a romance with one of its actresses. Rock Hudson's studio Universal put him together with Mamie van Doren.

Above: Lupe Velez – 'the Mexican Spitfire' – with her husband, *Tarzan* actor Johnny Weissmuller in 1935. In 1944, divorced and ashamed at being pregnant out of wedlock, Velez wrote a suicide note to her boyfriend, took an overdose of sedatives and killed herself.

for future election days. According to screenwriter Budd Schulberg, district attorney Buron Fitts 'was completely in the pocket of the producers'. And when politicians, the police, the Press and the law weren't being charmed by the glamour of Hollywood, they were being paid off by the studios.

Strickling worked with Eddie Mannix, Louis B. Mayer's general manager, who'd begun as a carnival bouncer for brothers Nicholas and Joseph Schenck at New York's Paradise amusement park. When the Schencks had moved into movies and co-created MGM, they took Mannix with them to keep an eye on Mayer.

Lavender Marriage

Of all the studios, MGM put the greatest value in creating stars. It therefore also had its work cut out protecting these stars, often from themselves. When actor William Haines was arrested with a sailor at a YMCA in 1933, Mannix and Strickling managed to hush the story up. But Mayer had had enough. He offered Haines the option of a 'lavender marriage' – a fake marriage to silence rumours about his sexuality – but Haines decided against it: he'd remain with his long-term boyfriend Jimmie Shields. Soon after that Haines found himself dropped by the studio. Giving up acting, he remained in Hollywood and made a successful second career as an interior designer to the stars.

Similarly, following well-founded rumours that Rock Hudson was gay, Universal Pictures invented a romance between him and another Universal contract player, the curvaceous Mamie van Doren. 'I think they used me to make people say, "Well, if he's going out with *her*, he certainly isn't gay,"' said van Doren.

> Strickling, it's alleged, had to pay out many times to keep photographs of a knickerless Velez from being circulated.

Hush Money

But what to do about a wronged wife? While *Tarzan* actor Johnny Weissmuller was married to singer Bobbe Arnst, his first of five wives, he began an affair with actress Lupe Velez. To protect Weissmuller, who was an MGM prize asset, Strickling paid Arnst $10,000 to go away. Weissmuller soon married Velez, but she was a heavy drinker who would end up dancing wildly at parties and lifting her skirt. Strickling, it's alleged, had to pay out many times to keep photographs of a knickerless Velez from being circulated. Similarly, it's also Hollywood folklore that Joan Crawford starred in a pornographic film before she was famous. When she became well-known, MGM, through money and Mob connections, managed to suppress the film from reaching the public – but saved it for after-dinner screenings at the homes of MGM executives.

Below: Spencer Tracy and Katharine Hepburn began a relationship in 1942 while making *Woman of the Year* (pictured). Their affair lasted until he died 25 years later, but as he was married, MGM kept the romance secret.

All in the Family

Louis B. Mayer liked to refer to his staff at MGM as his 'children' and the studio as a 'family'. If so, it was a really rather incestuous one. When Ingrid Bergman began an affair with Spencer Tracy, it wasn't just her husband, Petter Aron Lindström, who was upset, but director Victor Fleming. Why? Because he'd been having an affair with Bergman, too. Still, it was Lindström who took the matter to Mayer. The affair was duly stopped with Mannix threatening to fire Tracy. Tracy, of course, was also married, but he soon embarked on a 25-year affair with Katharine Hepburn. Strickling, subsequently, went to great lengths to keep that affair quiet, too.

> When Ingrid Bergman began an affair with Spencer Tracy, it wasn't just her husband, Petter Aron Lindström, who was upset …

Smile for the Cameras

Given his busy sex life, Clark Gable was one of MGM's most problematic stars. He'd arrived in Hollywood with his first wife Josephine Dillon, who'd been his acting coach and was more than ten years his senior. But by 1930, as Gable's career began to take off, the marriage was over and Gable moved in with wealthy Ria Langham, who was 17 years his senior. It didn't stop there. He was already having an affair with Joan Crawford, who was now pregnant, probably by Gable. He'd agreed to marry her, but then she wasn't actually available: she was married to Douglas Fairbanks Jr.

Distraught at her husband's adultery, Ria Langham approached MGM, threatening to expose all of Gable's affairs. Gable, reminded that he was in breach of the 'moral turpitude' clause of his contract, quickly put his house in order: forgetting his promise to wed Crawford, he agreed to marry Langham. That still left Crawford's pregnancy to deal with, so Strickling arranged for an abortion.

Gable might have been newly wed, but he was continuing to see Crawford, albeit discreetly. Nervous that Langham might still expose him, MGM forced Crawford and Fairbanks into a second honeymoon. Making a fuss of it, the studio staged a parade of police cars and well-wishers to see the couple off. Gable and Langham, meanwhile, were sent on a press tour of America to make their marriage as public as possible, too. Then, as punishment for his behaviour, Gable was relegated to a series of B-movies.

Suicide Whitewash

The studios could keep quiet stories about stars bedhopping, but what if the story was the naked corpse of a Hollywood figure?

When Howard Hughes gave Jean Harlow her break in *Hell's Angels* in 1930 even he said she had 'a voice like a Missouri barmaid screaming for a keg'. But she was cute. 'It doesn't matter what degree of talent she possesses,' wrote *Variety Magazine* of Harlow on the film's release, 'nobody ever starved possessing what she's got.' Her career was soon flagging, however, until in 1932, when aged 21, she married MGM producer Paul Bern. He was more than 20 years older than Harlow, but he managed to get her a contract at his studio.

Then, two months after their wedding, a naked Bern was found shot dead at their Beverly Hills home. Harlow was away visiting her mother at the time, but the butler, on finding the body, knew the protocol. He first called Strickling, who arrived with Mannix and Irving Thalberg, MGM's head of production. A suicide note was found that read: 'Dearest Dear, Unfortunately, this is the only way to make good the frightful wrong I have done you and to wipe out my abject humiliation. I love you, Paul... You understand that last night was only a comedy.'

Was this a genuine suicide note or just a peace-making message from an earlier marital falling-out? It's been suggested that Strickling and others found the message among Bern's things and planted it as a suicide note. The MGM heads all knew that Bern was,

> Joan Crawford was now pregnant, probably by Gable. He'd agreed to marry her, but then she wasn't actually available: she was married to Douglas Fairbanks Jr.

HOLLYWOOD'S MOST FAMOUS LOVE CHILD

WHILE FILMING *The Call of the Wild* in 1935, Clark Gable had an affair with Catholic co-star Loretta Young. She became pregnant and when it became too conspicuous to hide, MGM sent her on a long holiday to England. The love child, Judy, was born in secret at Young's home and brought up in an orphanage until she was 18 months old, when Young announced that she was going to adopt the girl. Not many people in Hollywood believed Young wasn't the child's natural mother.

While Gable was alive, Judy never knew that he was her father and only met him twice. However, as a young child she did have ears that stuck out just like her father's. To hide this, Loretta Young would make Judy wear bonnets whenever she was being photographed. When the girl was seven, Young decided Judy should have plastic surgery to pin her ears back. The surgeon warned that it'd be a very painful operation on a child so young. 'He suggested it should wait until I was older,' wrote Judy. 'But she insisted.'

Despite hearing rumours throughout her childhood that Gable was her father, it wasn't until the eve of her wedding, when she was 23, that Judy was told by her fiancé that the rumours were true. Judy confronted her mother, who admitted the truth, calling Judy 'a walking, mortal sin'.

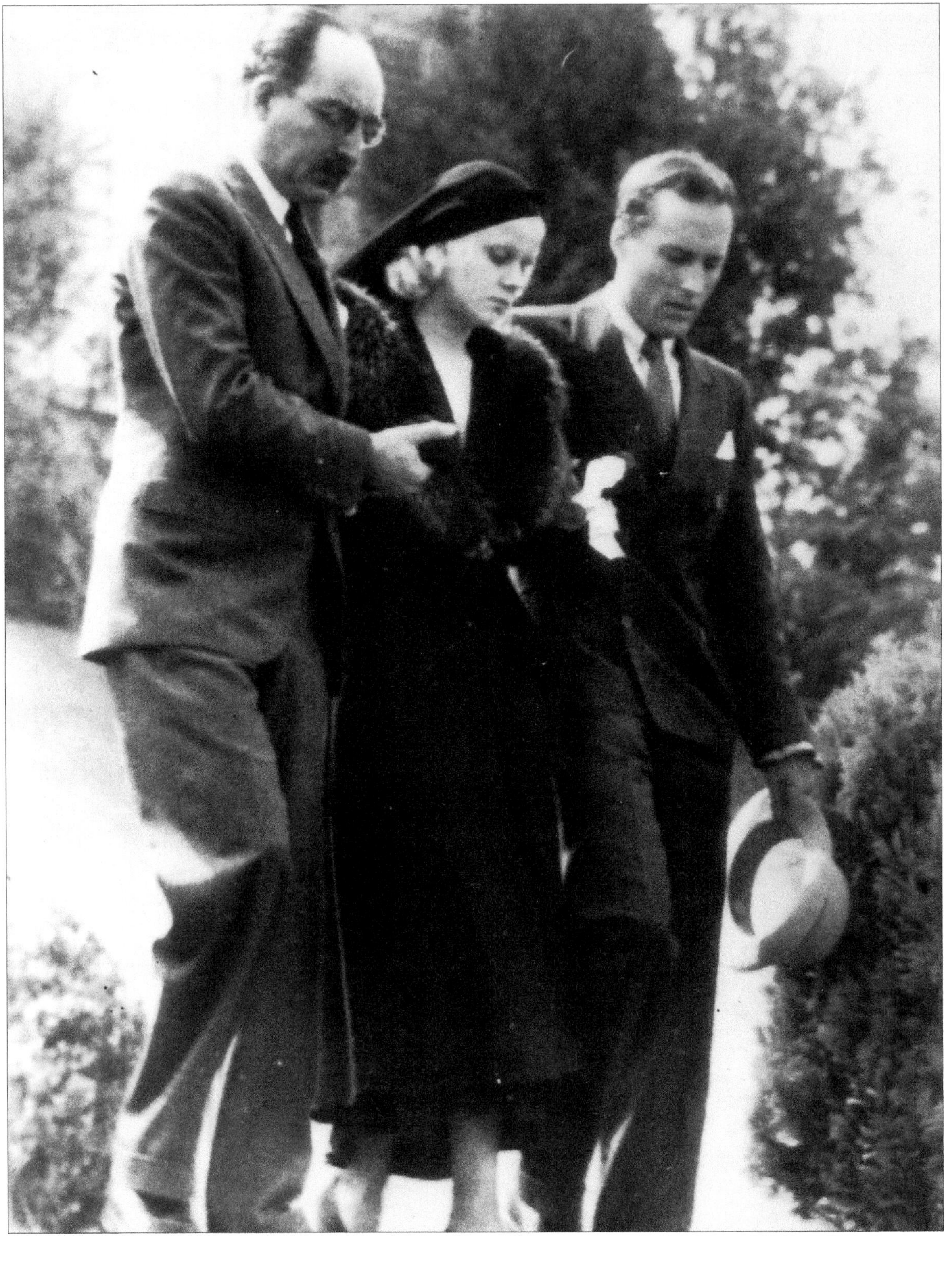

LANA'S HAWAII 500

LANA TURNER'S MARRIAGE to bandleader Artie Shaw lasted three months in 1939–40 before she threw him out. However, by then she was pregnant. For this, Louis B. Mayer was ready to fire her from MGM, but Eddie Mannix persuaded him against it and instead arranged an abortion for Turner, disguised as a 'publicity tour' to Hawaii. Mannix then deducted the $500 cost of the Hawaii trip from Turner's wages.

in fact, still married to actress Dorothy Millette (he'd married her 20 years earlier), but that their relationship had fallen apart after she'd had a mental breakdown.

Left: Jean Harlow, accompanied by relatives, at the funeral of her husband, Paul Bern. When their butler had found Bern shot dead, he'd first called MGM before ringing the police. Although ruled a suicide, doubt has always surrounded the circumstances of Bern's death.

If the suicide story is to be believed, Bern's 'abject humiliation' refers to his inability to perform sexually. But that doesn't explain everything. Although this line of enquiry wasn't pursued, a veiled woman – possibly Bern's real wife Dorothy Millette – had been seen arriving at the house the previous evening and an argument had followed. Bern's brother quickly began protesting that he didn't believe the suicide story, but once he'd seen Strickling he calmed down. Had he been bought off? Harlow never made any comment about the circumstances of Bern's death. A week later, Dorothy Millette jumped off a ferry in San Francisco Bay.

The coroner ruled a verdict of suicide, but many didn't believe the story. Even Samuel Marx, MGM's senior story editor at the time of Bern's death, later wrote a book arguing that Dorothy Millette, a wronged, troubled wife, had pulled the trigger. As screenwriter Budd Schulberg said: 'The studio heads were running a whole little world … they could cover up a murder.'

To Please Men

To young women, moving to Hollywood offered the hope of fame and a career in motion pictures, but if it didn't work out, Tinseltown must have seemed merely tawdry. While the girls might reasonably have thought that being signed up by a studio was the beginning of their movie careers, studios actually kept a group of young women on hand just for the entertainment of film exhibitors and visiting dignitaries. If these girls ever received any acting work, it was as extras. After six months, their contracts were seldom renewed. Hollywood had had its fun and moved on. To the studio there were plenty of pretty girls around trying to make it in Hollywood. They could refresh the crop.

When Joan Fontaine was about 18, she was asked to join some exhibitors on location. 'My mother went with me and sat at my table,' she said, 'and all of them came around and said, "Get rid of her."' Her mother soon ushered her off to bed, where, during the night, Fontaine ignored knocks at her door. Summoned the following day to see the studio head of publicity, Fontaine was reprimanded for being ungracious towards the businessmen. When her mother later complained to the studio, Fontaine wasn't asked to meet any businessmen again.

The Party Favour

Joan Fontaine got away, but dancer Patricia Douglas was less fortunate. When the 20-year-old responded to an MGM casting call in 1937, she thought it was for the usual chorus line work. Along with 120 other dancers and women who'd answered advertisements for 'MGM party hostesses', she was dressed in a cowboy hat, short suedette skirt and black boots, and bussed off to a remote studio property.

In fact, she hadn't been hired for a film, but to be part of the entertainment for MGM's three-day convention for salesmen. Promised a Wild West show 'stag affair', the salesmen considered the room of comely cowgirls as a 'party favour'. Although the early evening included appearances from Laurel & Hardy, later the event became increasingly debauched. 'The party was the worst, the wildest, and the rottenest I have ever seen,' said Henry Schulte, a waiter, in a later affidavit. 'The men's attitude was very rough. They were running their hands over the girls' bodies.'

> When the 20-year-old responded to an MGM casting call in 1937, she thought it was for the usual chorus line work.

Throughout the evening, David Ross, a salesman from Chicago, pursued Patricia Douglas. Later, he and another salesman pinned her down, pouring champagne and scotch into her mouth. When she escaped outside, Ross followed her and forced her into the back seat of a car, where, she claimed, he raped her. A parking attendant, Clement Soth, heard screams and saw her staggering towards him as Ross ran away.

Douglas was taken to Culver City Community Hospital, which, directly across from MGM, kept close ties to the studio. But before the doctor examined her, she was given a cold-water douche. 'It's no surprise he didn't find anything,' she said years later. 'The douche had removed all evidence.' No crime scene report was made, despite the police being aware of the rape allegation.

Douglas swore a complaint against Ross at the Los Angeles County district attorney's office. The DA, though, was Buron Fitts, who was very close with MGM's Louis B. Mayer. Hearing nothing from Fitts, Douglas engaged lawyer William J.F. Brown, who took her case on a pro bono basis. When Fitts also ignored Brown, Douglas went to the *Los Angeles Examiner*, which ran her story, although it didn't name the studio.

Right: Sent by her studio, RKO, to meet some lecherous exhibitors on location, a young Joan Fontaine took her mother to deter them. She was later reprimanded by the studio for her unfriendliness.

STANWYCK'S SUICIDE ATTEMPT

WHEN BARBARA STANWYCK slit her wrists because her actor husband Robert Taylor was having an affair with Lana Turner, Taylor first called Strickling, before taking Stanwyck to hospital. That way, when reports began to spread from the hospital, Strickling could have the story ready that Stanwyck had cut her wrists closing a window. When Turner herself attempted suicide in 1952, Strickling put out the story that she'd cut herself when she slipped in the shower.

> Ross's lawyer had been provided by MGM. 'Look at her,' he said, pointing at Patricia Douglas in court. 'Who would want her?'

At this point, the studio did respond, although perhaps not as one might expect. It hired the Pinkerton Detective Agency to track down all the girls who'd been at the party to make sure they toed the line. Statements were taken defending the party as 'clean fun' and describing Douglas as a lush, even though she'd been a teetotal virgin up until the night of the Wild West show.

When Douglas had no problem identifying Ross in photographs, Fitts was forced to convene a grand jury to determine if charges should be brought. At the hearing, only two of the girls would speak up in defence of Douglas, and Ross's lawyer, provided by MGM and a partner of Mayer's personal attorney, took a very mean line. 'Look at her,' he said, pointing to Patricia Douglas. 'Who would want her?' Worse, Clement Soth, the parking attendant who'd seen Ross running away from Douglas, now claimed that Ross wasn't the man. Years later Soth's daughters confirmed that MGM had offered him 'any job he wanted' if he perjured himself. Soth joined the MGM 'family' as a driver, remaining there for the rest of his working life.

The grand jury didn't indict David Ross, but Douglas didn't give up, pursuing the matter through two further courts. However, when Brown, her lawyer,

vowed to challenge Buron Fitts in the next election to be DA, a conflict of interest was thrown up. Brown didn't stand a chance of winning the election if he was in litigation with MGM, which was LA County's biggest employer. Around this time, Brown stopped appearing at Douglas's court hearings. Was he paid off by MGM? Or did he just realize that Douglas's case was an obstacle in his ambition to gain public office? Either way, with lawyers not attending Douglas's hearings, the case was dismissed. And Brown went on to lose against Fitts in the DA elections.

In handling the Patricia Douglas case, both MGM and the DA's office had begun by doing as little as possible, apparently in the hope that she'd just go away. Then, when forced into action, MGM had gone to a great deal of effort to defend itself. The Wild West party scandal was front-page news at the time, but it quickly faded from Hollywood histories, only resurfacing when author David Stenn investigated Douglas's story for *Vanity Fair* magazine in 2003. Speaking for the first time about the rape that year, Douglas said: 'It absolutely ruined my life.'

Blackballed

Patricia Douglas had been a nobody in the studio's eyes before the rape allegation, but even established names had their run-ins. One evening in a restaurant, Louis B. Mayer made a pass at Esther Ralston, who had been a star in the silent era and was under contract at MGM. She politely rebuffed him and thought nothing more of it. But the following morning she was summoned to his office. 'You think you're pretty smart, don't you?' Mayer said, surprising her. 'Well, I'll blackball you. You'll never get another picture in any studio in town.'

Actually, Mayer didn't blackball her, but Ralston knew then that her career at MGM was over. Mayer

Left: Barbara Stanwyck with Robert Taylor in Venice in the 1950s. When she discovered his affair with Lana Turner, Stanwyck slit her wrists, but MGM quickly told the Press that she'd cut herself opening a window.

took no further interest in her career, loaning her out to Universal for 13 films *in a row*. MGM received a commission each week from Universal for Ralston, while Universal paid her weekly income. Relegated to smaller roles, she made her final film in 1940, aged 38, before retiring from cinema. It hadn't paid to reject the head of the studio's advances.

Married but Looking

The studios had such control over their stars' lives that it became second nature to consult them on matters unrelated to their work. When Ava Gardner accepted

Mickey Rooney's marriage proposal, his first response was: 'Great. Who are we going to break the news to first – Ma or Uncle L.B. [Mayer]?' They tossed a coin for it. Ma won.

Mayer, however, wasn't happy when he heard the news. Rooney, at 21, was still playing wholesome teenage roles in the Andy Hardy films and Mayer

Below: While Ava Gardner had imagined MGM organizing a lavish Beverly Hills spectacle for her wedding to its biggest star, the studio didn't want to upset Mickey Rooney's teenage girl fans. Instead, it arranged a quiet ceremony in a tiny town 120 miles outside LA.

APPEASING NAZI GERMANY

EVEN WHEN IT came to Nazi Germany, the Hollywood studios were open for business, revealed Ben Urwand in his 2013 book *The Collaboration: Hollywood's Pact with Hitler.* In 1933, screenwriter Herman J. Mankiewicz offered a topical script about the treatment of Jews in Nazi Germany around Hollywood, but he couldn't find a backer. Regarding the project, Louis B. Mayer said: 'We have terrific income in Germany ... as far as I am concerned, this picture will never be made.' It wasn't just that Hollywood feared certain films being unpopular in Germany. According to a pre-Nazi amendment to the German film regulations, if a studio released an anti-German film anywhere in the world, all films from that studio could be banned in Germany. As the Nazi government became more extreme, it took the amendment increasingly seriously, while the studios took the German market seriously, too.

As a wider consequence of this amendment, the studios consulted Georg Gyssling, the German Consul in LA from 1933 and a Nazi Party member, allowing him to list the cuts that he wanted made to a film before it was distributed. If Gyssling (pictured with Leni Riefenstahl, best known for her Nazi propaganda documentaries) felt there was criticism of modern Germany in a film, such as German anti-Semitism or militarism, the studios usually bowed to his wishes and made the relevant cuts. For as long as the studios cared about the German market, a Nazi Party member in LA was censoring Hollywood films.

Many of the studio heads were Jewish, but they were businessmen first, pitching their films to as wide an audience as possible. As Columbia Pictures head Harry Cohn said: 'Around this studio, the only Jews we put into pictures play Indians!' Nor were the studios interested in issues-based films – as Harry Warner famously said: 'We should leave messages to Western Union.'

Not that the moguls were insensitive to anti-Semitism. When they'd first arrived in Los Angeles, Jews had been barred from the country clubs and had set up their own, Hillcrest – where they had the last laugh when oil was discovered beneath the greens in 1950. They weren't inactive either: Carl Laemmle, the German-born Jewish head of Universal, helped almost 300 German Jews escape persecution and find passage to America.

As the Nazi Government demanded greater and greater cuts from American films (or simply banned them altogether) in the later 1930s, the Hollywood studios began to pull out of Germany – it was no longer worth their trouble. And with MGM and Fox producing anti-Nazi films in 1940, the last two US studios were finally expelled from Germany.

wanted him to remain single and available in the eyes of his young fans. Mayer even tried to dissuade Rooney from marrying Gardner, but, failing in that, he settled for a policy of damage limitation and quickly began organizing a quiet wedding out of town and away from the Press. Not consulting the couple on whether the wedding arrangements were any of MGM's business, an MGM publicist even accompanied them on their honeymoon.

Because of Rooney's philandering, however, their marriage was soon in trouble. 'He'd screw anything that moved,' said Gardner. The breaking point came at a nightclub where Rooney produced his little black book of girls, and, in front of Gardner, began reading out what each girl was particularly good at in bed. Gardner left him, MGM persuading her not to sue for divorce on the grounds of adultery but simply incompatibility: there'd be less bad press that way. Perhaps it was unrelated, but at the same time Gardner's contract was renewed and she was given a rise.

Who Killed Superman?

A fatal shooting, a wealthy, older Hollywood woman and her younger lover seeking escape – that's 1950's *Sunset Boulevard*, isn't it? It is, but nine years later life imitated art. And for all the scandals that Eddie Mannix had been drawn into, this one concerned him personally.

By the late 1930s, Mannix was living apart from his first wife Bernice. She was preparing to divorce him, accusing him of cruelty, of beating her severely enough to break her back and of committing adultery with Toni Lanier, a former Ziegfeld Follies dancer. Mannix could afford his wife's hefty alimony, but could he afford Toni's spending needs on top of that? It's claimed that, in November 1937, through organized crime contacts, Mannix had Bernice's car run off the road, killing her

> The breaking point came at a nightclub where Rooney produced his little black book of girls, and, in front of Gardner, began reading out what each girl was particularly good at in bed.

> Just as Bernice Maddix's car had been run off the road, Reeves's car was nearly pushed into a ravine and his brakes were cut.

before she could file her divorce papers. After that, Mannix set up home with Toni and, although they never formally married, she became known as 'Mrs Mannix'. By 1951, Mannix was in his late fifties and had heart trouble. He openly had a Japanese mistress, and didn't object when Toni, in her mid-forties, began seeing actor George Reeves, ten years her junior. The four of them even dined out together.

Despite an earlier role in *Gone with the Wind*, Reeves had struggled throughout the 1940s. With Toni, though, things began to brighten. He let her buy him a house, and the same year – perhaps with help from Mannix – Reeves was cast as Superman in the television serial *The Adventures of Superman*. For Reeves, children's television was definitely a step down, but the show became a hit, making him rich and famous.

Toni had assumed that she and Reeves would marry after Mannix had died, although he'd now survived several heart attacks. But, over the years, as Reeves's star rose, the balance in his relationship with Toni changed. He now had fans and admirers. In 1958, after seven years with Toni, he began an affair with Leonore Lemmon, a 38-year-old party girl. Breaking off the relationship with Toni, Reeves was soon engaged to Lemmon.

Given that Eddie Mannix was a powerful man whose first wife had died in suspicious circumstances and who had beaten up previous girlfriends, but who'd accepted Reeves's relationship with Toni, it might have seemed reckless for Reeves to discard Toni so casually. Would Mannix allow his wife to be humiliated and hurt like that? Perhaps not. Strange things began to happen to Reeves. Just as Bernice Mannix's car had been run off the road, Reeves's car was nearly pushed into a ravine. On another occasion, his brakes had been

Right: George Reeves and Lucille Ball photographed during his guest appearance on *I Love Lucy* in 1957. Playing Superman on TV had brought Reeves fame and wealth, but some said that he was depressed, feeling shackled to the role.

cut and he'd crashed, his body being thrown through the windscreen. While a heartbroken Toni was trying to win him back, Reeves's relationship with Lemmon was falling apart as she maintained a status of constant partying. Then one night in his bedroom in June 1959, while Leonore Lemmon and guests held a party downstairs, Reeves shot himself.

Or did he? Although the death was declared a suicide, evidence suggested that the gun that killed him had been at some distance, rather than pressed to his

Above: Leonore Lemmon, Reeves's fiancée, leaving his house after his death on 16 June 1959. As the actor had gone to bed the previous night, she was said to have commented: 'He's going up there to kill himself.'

head. There were two other bullet holes in the floor of his bedroom, too. Would a suicide have missed that badly? And there were bruises on him, indicating that there'd been a struggle.

Only after a 45-minute delay had the police been

BUSBY BERKELEY'S SHARP MOVES

ONE NIGHT IN 1935, choreographer Busby Berkeley was driving home from a party along the Pacific Coast Highway when he veered across the road and crashed into two oncoming cars. Three people were killed, and two more were seriously injured (one later died), while Berkeley escaped with cuts and bruises. Berkeley called

Whitey Hendry, head of MGM's head of security, and Hendry called Jerry Giesler. At the court hearing, in what would seem to be a piece of theatre, Berkeley was wheeled in wrapped in bandages. Giesler's defence was that Berkeley's tyre had burst and he'd lost control of the car. But Berkeley had a reputation as a drinker, and, although he'd denied drinking that night, witnesses at the crash scene said that he'd been speeding and that he smelt of alcohol. After the first two juries were divided and mistrials were called, the third jury acquitted Berkeley. He returned to work and MGM later paid out $100,000 in civil damages to the families of those killed and injured. If Berkeley hadn't been a celebrity with a top lawyer, would he have been acquitted?

Reeves shot himself. Or did he? Although the death was declared a suicide, evidence suggested that the gun that killed him had been at some distance, rather than pressed to his head.

called. Lemmon and her guests all gave the same, drunken, story. When they'd heard the gunshot, Bill Bliss, who neither Reeves nor Lemmon knew, had been sent upstairs to investigate and had returned shouting 'My friend is dead!' The police didn't take any fingerprints and interviewed all the witnesses together, rather than separating them.

Reeves's mother, Helen Bessolo, was convinced that her son had been murdered and brought in Hollywood lawyer Jerry Giesler to investigate further. Giesler,

CITIZEN KANE

AS ACTOR AND director, Orson Welles was the 'boy genius' of 1930s New York radio and theatre. When he was not yet 25, Hollywood beckoned. Joining forces with screenwriter Herman J. Mankiewicz, Welles directed *Citizen Kane*, a film that, although it was presented as fiction, clearly mirrored, and at times lampooned, the life of America's richest living newspaper tycoon, William Randolph Hearst. Mankiewicz had been a journalist for Hearst newspapers and had known him socially before being barred for drunkenness. But could the cynical wit Mankiewicz and the cocky Welles get away with mocking a man as powerful as Hearst?

RKO Pictures backed *Citizen Kane*, but shortly before the film's proposed release on Valentine's Day 1941, Hearst banned advertisements or articles related to any RKO films in his newspapers. So, what did Hearst object to in the film? It's been suggested that while he was thick-skinned enough to take the flak about his business life, he was sensitive about the portrayal of newspaper baron Charles Foster Kane as senile (Hearst was 78 when the film was made).

More importantly, the film mocked Kane's love for a much younger lounge singer, whom he fails to turn into an opera star. Hearst's girlfriend, actress Marion Davies, was 40 years younger than he was, and never became a star, despite the contracts set up for her at MGM and Warners after Hearst bought stock in the companies. And Davies, like Kane's lover, had a drink problem.

On seeing a preview of the film, Louella Parsons, the gossip columnist on Hearst's *Los Angeles Examiner,* threatened Welles (pictured, right, as Kane) and the RKO board of directors that she'd write fictitious scandals about them if *Citizen Kane* was released. The movie was booked to première at Radio City Music Hall in New York, but when the manager was threatened that no Hearst newspaper would ever again review or accept advertising for a film that played there, he turned his back on it. Bowing to pressure, the RKO board agreed to delay the film's release, while major news agencies dropped *Citizen Kane* stories. They couldn't afford to have Hearst newspapers stop buying their material.

Hearst also began calling in favours. He reminded Louis B. Mayer of all the times his newspapers hadn't run scandals they'd uncovered about MGM's stars, or had given weak films good coverage. It's not clear if it was Hearst money or Hollywood money, but Mayer subsequently offered to buy *Citizen Kane* off RKO so that it could be destroyed. RKO turned him down.

When the movie was finally released in May 1941, some cinema circuits wouldn't accept it, fearing lawsuits or losing advertising space in Hearst newspapers. RKO later sent it out as part of their block-booking package of films, but many cinemas simply chose not to screen it and took a loss. And, despite good reviews, the public didn't flock to the available screenings.

Citizen Kane went on to be nominated for nine Oscars, winning for Mankiewicz's and Welles's screenplay, and, in time, it would often be voted the greatest film ever made. Hearst hadn't stopped the picture, but he'd hurt it at the box office. Hollywood studios were powerful, but Hearst was bigger. *Citizen Kane* paid the price for making fun of William Randolph Hearst.

who'd represented mobster Bugsy Siegel, backed out of the case, telling Bessolo that there were too many dangerous people involved. Toni Mannix also didn't think it was suicide. She made a phone call a couple of hours after Reeves's death, telling a friend he'd been murdered. After that, Mannix kept her sedated for weeks and she was never interviewed by police.

If it wasn't suicide, had Leonore Lemmon shot Reeves in a drunken struggle? Or was it done on behalf of broken-hearted Toni? Or on behalf of Mannix for the pain it was causing Toni and the embarrassment it was causing him? Was it a case of murder dressed as suicide, as people suspect Paul Bern's death might have been 25 years earlier? After all, when Bern's butler had discovered his body, it was Strickling and Mannix he rang first.

The Stars Fight Back

When it came to money, even the biggest stars sometimes had to resort to some extreme measures to better their deal. James Cagney managed to lever Warner Bros. up from $1000 to $1750 a week in 1932 by walking out on the studio. But when he tried this again in the late 1930s, Warners took him to court, simultaneously using their clout to limit the distribution of two films Cagney had made independently. The studio's influence may have reached further than Cagney had anticipated. Chastened, he returned to his old studio.

When Bette Davis turned down two scripts in a row in 1937, Warners put her on a three-month suspension without pay. She headed to Britain, planning to make films in Europe, but Warners responded by serving her with an injunction, prohibiting her from working anywhere. From London, Davis sued the studio, but became aware that she was, in fact, taking on the whole system. 'Not one other film company in Hollywood would touch me with a ten-foot pole,' she later wrote, 'for, were I to win the case, every major star would rush for the nearest exit and follow me to freedom.' She failed in her lawsuit, but Jack Warner subsequently paid her legal fees and began giving her better roles. Unlike that of Cagney, her fight had paid off.

Left: The première of *Citizen Kane* in May 1941. A number of Hearst sympathizers had even begun reporting Welles's activities to the FBI as being potentially dangerous to the national interest. An investigation into the star was launched, though nothing came of it.

Below: Although she was being paid $1350 a week in 1937, Bette Davis called working for Jack Warner 'slavery' and sued the studio. But when she was then blacklisted by all the other studios, she was forced to back down.

And Davis wasn't the only one. Following an Oscar-nominated role in 1939's *Gone with the Wind*, Olivia de Havilland was disappointed to be only offered middling scripts by Warner Bros. Having begun to turn down roles, she was placed on suspension. Rather than caving in, she took her case to the Superior Court of California, citing the law that limited employment contracts to seven years. The court hearings lasted for months and, unable to work, she didn't appear on screen for two years. However, in March 1944, the court ruled that actors were released from serving out time added to their contracts through suspensions. De Havilland had won. The hold of the studio system had begun to weaken.

> In 1946, cinema attendances had reached an all-time high of 98 million, but by 1950 this had plunged to 50 million.

End of an Era

Four years later the studios would be dealt another blow. During the golden age, the studios had come to not only produce and distribute their movies, but also to own 80 per cent of 'first run' cinemas, taking in 45 per cent of the US box office. They'd achieved some of this by using the threat of physical violence to muscle out the weaker competition, and when they didn't own the cinemas, they'd insist on blind-bidding and block-booking. Thus, independent cinemas weren't given a chance to view films before ordering them, and if a cinema wanted a prized film, it had to take a dozen poorer movies in the same package. In all, the studios maintained an anti-competitive hold over the cinema chains.

Although lawsuits to break this had begun in 1933, the studios managed to keep their system going legally through the courts and illegally through pay-offs. But in 1948 the Supreme Court ruled that they had to sell off their cinemas. They'd lost the direct access to

Left: Olivia de Havilland, who had co-starred in *Gone with the Wind*, successfully sued Warner Bros. when it added six months of suspension time to her seven-year contract. She changed Hollywood, too – seven years became the absolute maximum by law.

the box office and the immense collateral wealth of all their cinemas. The movie moguls who'd been the cinema-owning upstarts and had challenged Edison's cartel were now being separated from their cinemas for running their own cartel.

Show Me the Money

Having broken the hold over long contracts, stars now pushed for greater freedom. On returning to Hollywood after serving as a bomber pilot during World War II, James Stewart followed his agent Lew Wasserman's advice and worked independently, rather than committing to another long studio contract. And when Stewart made *Winchester '73* in 1950, Wasserman negotiated for him a first in Hollywood: Stewart would give up his fee for the film in return for a percentage of the film's profits. When the film went on to be a hit and Stewart made $600,000, all the stars wanted profit participation. After a generation of what some actors had described as 'slavery' under the studio system, stars were once again in a position to bargain.

The entire Hollywood landscape was changing. The moguls were wily showmen who went on gut instinct, but they weren't actually very good at numbers and certainly weren't men of corporate finance. Now the likes of Lew Wasserman were bringing a more corporate nous to Hollywood itself, and it was undermining the studio system.

Changing Times

Beyond the concerns of Hollywood politics, America itself was transforming. In 1946, cinema attendances had reached an all-time high of 98 million, but by 1950 this had plunged to 50 million. With a post-war population boom, young adults were spending their money moving to the suburbs, where there weren't cinemas, and investing in their new houses and families

> Stewart would give up his fee in return for a percentage of the film's profits. When the film went on to be a hit and Stewart made $600,000, all the stars wanted profit participation.

Above: In *Winchester '73* James Stewart broke the Hollywood mould in not being paid an upfront fee. Instead, he had a percentage of the film's profits, which also enabled him to avoid 90 per cent tax rates.

rather than going out. And, from the late 1940s, into those suburban homes came television.

Initially, the moguls regarded television as an immense threat, even prohibiting TV sets being seen in their films. They were also surprisingly short-sighted: when the live broadcast rights to the Academy Awards ceremony were sold to television in 1953, the studios still held the event on a Saturday evening – the biggest movie-going night of the week. After that, *Daily Variety* suggested that, 'Hollywood return the art of hara-kiri to the Japanese'. These days the Oscars are held on Sundays.

By the mid-1950s, MGM, which 20 years earlier had promised 'more stars than there are in heaven',

was the last studio to cease keeping actors on contracts. Audiences could no longer recognize a studio by its actors and the moguls were moving on or growing old. Agents were becoming more powerful, although even they probably couldn't yet imagine that in another ten years Lew Wasserman's agency MCA would buy Universal Pictures.

'Hollywood's like Egypt,' said studio head David O. Selznick in the early 1950s, 'full of crumbling pyramids. It'll never come back. It'll just keep crumbling until finally the wind blows the last studio prop across the sands.' He was right about the studio system, but wrong about Hollywood.

Right: Bob Hope was the master of ceremonies at the first televised Academy Awards in 1953. At different stages, the studios had both ignored, resented and feared television, but, in time, they came to embrace it as another way of making money from movies.

THE BLACKLIST

The anti-Communist witch-hunts of the 1940s and 1950s ruined careers, tore friendships apart, forced some film-makers to leave America for good, and perhaps even caused some early deaths. But how could that have happened? What led America into blacklisting more than 300 people working in Hollywood? Were film-makers really inserting Communist propaganda into movies? And was there really a planned Communist takeover of Hollywood?

◆

'Have you ever been a member of the Communist Party?'

Although the post-war anti-Communist witch-hunts were products of the Cold War, their genesis in Hollywood can be found as early as the invention of talking pictures. From 1928, Hollywood demanded actors who could not only act well but speak as well, and that required writers who could come up with convincing dialogue for them. This brought to Hollywood an invasion of actors and playwrights from Broadway, where, not part of the

MGM's head of production Irving Thalberg, like many Americans of the 1930s, feared Communism more than Fascism. 'When a dictator dies,' he said, 'his system dies, too. But if Communism is allowed to spread, it will be harder to root out.'

studio system, they'd had their own unions, such as Actors Equity. Fearing unionization in their industry, the studios had established the Academy of Motion Picture Arts and Sciences in 1927, but in April 1933 the Screen Writers Guild (SWG) was set up in Los Angeles and hundreds joined.

MGM's head of production Irving Thalberg immediately tried to resist the power of the SWG. 'Those writers are living like kings,' he said. 'Why on earth would they want to join a union like coal miners or plumbers?' In fact, in that very year, 1933, in the middle of the Depression, the studios had declared they couldn't meet payroll and had cut the pay by half of any employees earning more than $50 a week – which included screenwriters. At first the studios said it would be only for two months, but they reneged on their promise and the lower rates remained.

Above: Budd Schulberg was born into a privileged Hollywood upbringing, became a screenwriter who joined the Communist Party for a time in the 1930s and later named names. This allowed him to continue working, but ruined some of his friendships.

The screenwriters' union wanted to ensure that writers were credited on the films they wrote, rather than sometimes seeing a studio favourite's name on the screen when he or she hadn't even been involved in the production.

The irony of the studios' battles with the SWG was that it probably made the screenwriters more politically aware than many had ever been. Budd Schulberg, for instance, who'd grown up in Hollywood, joined the Communist Party. 'Fascism was coming, the old world was dying, a new world would be born,' he would explain, while admitting to, 'some sense of guilt about being in Hollywood, living that prosperous life, knowing that millions of people were suffering in America, that unemployment was horrendous, and the whole world was sort of hurting.' Screenwriter Albert Hackett quipped: 'Louis B. Mayer created more Communists than Karl Marx.'

But how serious was membership of the Communist Party in 1930s southern California? 'In those years just before the war, the activity of the Communists in the Hollywood section was very little different from the left-wing liberals generally,' said screenwriter Ring Lardner Jr, referring to a group known as the Popular Front who were active in the Anti-Nazi League and the Motion Picture Democratic Committee. As writer Philip Dunne remembered: 'I think the Communists had a great deal to do with forming the organizations, but they did it purely on an anti-Nazi basis.'

Nor was the screenwriters' union only about arguing for better pay. It also wanted to ensure that writers were credited on the films they wrote, rather than sometimes seeing a studio favourite's name on the screen when he or she hadn't even been involved in the production. But, whether fighting for money or credit for their work, the battle between the SWG and the studios continued throughout the 1930s, as Roosevelt's New Deal promoted unionization across the country.

The studios' battles with the SWG probably made screenwriters more politically aware. Said writer Albert Hackett: 'Louis B. Mayer created more Communists than Karl Marx.'

'NOTHING IS UNFAIR IN POLITICS'

WHEN, IN 1934, novelist Upton Sinclair (pictured below) stood for election as Democrat governor of California and proposed higher taxes on the studios and on the rich, the studios quickly united behind acting Republican governor Frank E. Merriam. Newsreels were distributed that were very selectively edited so that of those interviewed, only the obviously well-to-do came out in favour of Merriam and the poor and dirty were used only if they were voting for Sinclair.

Further sullying of the Sinclair campaign came in the *Los Angeles Examiner,* which hired actors from Central Casting, dressed them as down and outs, and photographed them supposedly arriving in California on freight trains to cash in on Sinclair's 'End Poverty' campaign. In defence of these tactics, MGM's Irving Thalberg, who was allegedly behind the newsreels, said: 'Nothing is unfair in politics.' Merriam went on to win an overwhelming victory.

Red Scare

By 1936, the conservative trade newspaper the *Hollywood Reporter* had begun to link the SWG directly with Communism, while in the *Los Angeles Examiner,* press baron William Randolph Hearst described a proposal to amalgamate the SWG and other writers'

guilds (encompassing authors, playwrights and radio dramatists) as 'a device of Communist radicals'. And when some screenwriters began raising money for the Loyalists in the Spanish Civil War (1936–9), MGM's front office was so alarmed that Eddie Mannix placed a number of MGM's employees under surveillance.

Congressman Martin Dies claimed that members of the Anti-Nazi League were, at best, Communist dupes and Hollywood was a 'hotbed of Communism'.

Above: Dedicated to exposing Communist conspiracies, the Dies Committee was led by congressman Martin Dies (pictured sitting centre). It was established by an alliance of Republicans and Democrats united in their hostility to Roosevelt's New Deal.

Paranoia was being stoked. In 1938, Texas Congressman Martin Dies made a national radio broadcast in which he claimed that members of the Anti-Nazi League were, at best, Communist dupes, and

that he had a list of nearly 40 film personalities (which included Joan Crawford and Paul Muni), who were on record as contributors to what he loosely termed 'Communist causes'. Hollywood, he told the Press, was a 'hotbed of Communism'.

The following year, another of Dies's lists was leaked to the Press, stating that 40 Hollywood names, including Humphrey Bogart and James Cagney, were Communists. Actor Lionel Stander was on this list

> ' ... what they actually did was to attack anyone and everyone who supported Roosevelt's New Deal.'

and first appeared before the Dies Committee (the forerunner of the House Committee on Un-American Activities) in 1940. 'They gave me a clean bill of health,' he said later. 'I swore I wasn't a member of the Communist Party and had never been, and that was it ... They professed to investigate un-American activities but what they actually did was to attack anyone and everyone who supported Roosevelt's New Deal.'

Corruption in the Unions

As it turned out, everyone investigated by the Dies Committee was cleared to work, apart from Stander, who was fired. Why? The previous year he'd spoken out against corruption in the technicians' union, the International Association of Theatrical and Stage Employees (IATSE), and had cited the criminal records of its president, George E. Browne, and IATSE's Hollywood representative Willie Bioff (pronounced 'buy off'). IATSE was universally recognized by the studios, making it the most powerful union, but it was

Below: Lionel Stander and Virginia Dale in *No Time To Marry* (1938). Stander managed to get himself blacklisted, not for being a member of the Communist Party (he wasn't), but because he'd spoken out against the corruption of the studios.

also widely known that it was controlled by the Mafia through Browne and Bioff.

So, as a reward for speaking out, Stander's contract with Columbia wasn't renewed and Columbia's Harry Cohn stated that any studio that signed Stander would be subject to a $1000 fine from the Motion Pictures' Producers Association. From 1939, Stander went to work for independent producers.

Communist Europe

During the 1930s, Hollywood liberals had been actively anti-Fascist and anti-Nazi, but the 1939 Hitler-Stalin Pact, by which the forces of Fascism and Communism in Europe teamed up, surprised everyone. Now, being an idealistic supporter of Communist ideals of common ownership and equality (if not actual Soviet Communism) became tainted with supporting Hitler's aggressive expansionism and anti-Semitism in Europe. Furthermore, the Moscow show trials of 1936–8, where the old Bolshevik guard had been purged, exiled

Left: Herbert Sorrell established a rival union to IATSE in the Conference of Studio Unions (CSU). IATSE responded by accusing the CSU of being infiltrated by Communists. In turn IATSE was accused of being a studio front.

> The Red Scare intensified, and, in 1941, Walt Disney took out advertisements in the trade newspapers on the danger of Communist agitators behind an animator's strike.

or executed by Stalin, had revealed to the West an uglier side to Soviet Communism. As a result, the Red Scare intensified, and, in 1941, Walt Disney took out advertisements in the trade newspapers on the danger of Communist agitators behind an animator's strike.

But was the target really Communists or the unions? According to director Edward Dmytryk, 'The Hollywood Right-wing leaders wanted to stop the unions short.' While there had been Communists active in the SWG and several actors had briefly been Party members, Dmytryk reckoned there were only about eight directors in the Directors Guild who

Below: In the autumn of 1945, the Conference of Studio Unions called a strike of carpenters, set painters and other studio staff. Outside Warner Bros., the strike became violent, with armed police charging the picket lines.

were Communists and only 250 Communists in all Hollywood. (At its peak there were never more than 50,000 members of the Communist Party in the entire USA.)

US entry into World War II in 1941 led to a no-strike pledge by the unions, but in the autumn of 1945, a strike of carpenters, set painters and other studio staff turned violent outside Warner Bros. Armed police charged the picket lines, strikers fought back, fire hoses were turned on them and tear gas was used. Ronald Reagan, then president of the Screen Actors Guild, led actors in breaking the picket lines. Again, it was claimed that it wasn't just left-wing unions that were being defeated; Reagan went on record saying he'd 'headed off this Communist takeover plot', which, said writer Philip Dunne, 'was sheer, absolute eyewash – it never existed'. In response to this perceived threat in Hollywood, in 1947 Walt Disney co-founded the Motion Picture Alliance for the Preservation of American Ideals, a political action group that issued a pamphlet advising producers on the avoidance of

> Ronald Reagan went on record saying he'd 'headed off a Communist takeover plot,' which, said writer Philip Dunne, 'was sheer, absolute eyewash – it never existed'.

'subtle communistic touches' in their films by following a list of commandments: wealth, free enterprise, industrialists and the profit motive were not to be besmirched, while the common man and the collective weren't to be glorified.

Un-American Activities

Also in 1947, a more aggressive House Committee on Un-American Activities (HUAC), chaired by Republican J. Parnell Thomas of New Jersey, targeted Hollywood. Parnell had become convinced that recent strikes had been inspired by Communism and told

Below: John Parnell Thomas (second left) and members of the House Committee on Un-American Activities in 1948. Thomas himself later went to prison for corruption. Far right is the congressman for California and future President Richard Nixon.

Above: The Hollywood Ten in 1948. They were known as the 'unfriendly' witnesses because they'd refused to give evidence before the House Committee on Un-American Activities. They were ultimately given prison sentences for contempt of Congress.

the Motion Picture Association of America (MPAA) that every Communist employed in Hollywood should be dismissed because they were dedicated to the overthrow of the American government and were using their films to achieve this. The MPAA responded that they'd do no such thing, but the following month Jack Warner called for 'an all-out fight on the Commies'.

With the help of the FBI in gathering information (as Ronald Reagan was passing names to them, they were also tapping phone lines, including that of actor Edward G. Robinson), HUAC issued subpoenas to 43 Hollywood people. These were divided into two groups to appear at Committee hearings. The first group became known as 'friendly' witnesses because they were willing to name fellow Hollywood workers who were believed to be Communist Party members – most of whom were. Along with being asked if they had ever

> That reduced the group to ten, who became famously known as the Hollywood Ten, all members of the Communist Party.

been members of the Communist Party, witnesses were asked if they'd ever been members of the SWG, as if it were virtually the same thing.

The second group consisted of 19 writers, producers, directors and actors who were suspected of Communist sympathies. They became known as the 'unfriendly' witnesses. After preliminary hearings in Los Angeles, 11 of the 19 'unfriendly' witnesses were called to testify in Washington. German playwright Bertolt Brecht denied that he was a Communist and within hours flew back to Europe, settling in Communist East Germany. When Brecht left the US, that reduced the group to ten, who became famously known as the Hollywood Ten, all of whom had at one time been members of the Communist Party. They were, seven screenwriters: John Howard Lawson, Dalton Trumbo, Ring Lardner Jr, Alvah Bessie, Lester Cole, Samuel Ornitz and Albert Maltz; one producer: Adrian Scott; and two directors: Edward Dmytryk and Herbert Biberman.

Dmytryk had had a successful career, but once the pink subpoena arrived, his life, and those of the other members of the Hollywood Ten, changed. 'All of a sudden I was getting phone calls from my friends saying, "You're not going to continue going with this man are you?"', said Dmytryk's wife, actress Jean Porter. 'Some of his friends dropped away, some of my friends dropped away. He didn't believe for one minute that he would be fired, but both our careers were affected.'

A fightback against HUAC quickly began to take shape and many Hollywood names not directly under suspicion formed the Committee for the First Amendment.

During the HUAC hearings the 'unfriendly' 19 stayed at the Shoreham Hotel in Washington. 'No foreign city could have been more alien and hostile,' said their supporter, writer Howard Koch. 'All our hotel rooms were bugged. When we wanted to talk with each other, we had to either keep twirling a metal key to jam the circuit or go out of doors.'

Subversive Cinema?
Naturally, a fightback against HUAC quickly began to take shape and many Hollywood names not directly under suspicion, such as Humphrey Bogart, Lauren Bacall, Danny Kaye, John Huston and Philip Dunne, formed the Committee for the First Amendment, and all flew to Washington to protest at the undemocratic nature of HUAC.

'We were so angry that headline-hunting Congressmen would use Hollywood and motion pictures as a step to their own self-glorification,' said actress Marsha Hunt. Since the film-makers who had appeared before HUAC had been accused of

'It's crazy to think that I could have put propaganda into a film that the common man would understand but that the capitalists wouldn't.'

---

inserting Communist propaganda into their films, their supporters called press conferences to explain how difficult that would have been. 'You'd have to have been some kind of great magician to be able to get any real Communist propaganda into a film,' Edward Dmytryk later wrote, 'because the people who financed our pictures were the bankers, and they were all good one hundred percent American capitalists. It's crazy to think that I could have put propaganda into a film that the common man would understand but that the capitalists wouldn't. Besides, Communistic manifestos are very dull drama.'

Hollywood was divided. On the Right was Disney's Motion Picture Alliance for the Preservation of American Ideals, represented, among others, by Cecil B. DeMille, John Wayne and gossip columnist Hedda Hopper, and on the Left the Committee for the First Amendment. Many of the newspapers were highly critical of HUAC. 'We do not believe the committee is conducting a fair investigation,' read an editorial in the *New York Times*. 'We think the course upon which it is embarked threatens to lead to greater dangers than those with which it is presently concerned.' In fact, the hearings generated such bad publicity for HUAC that they were cut short, with eight of the 'unfriendly' 19 not being heard. That, however, did not improve things for the Hollywood Ten. 'Once we were subpoenaed,' Edward Dmytryk said, 'we were all broke within six months, because we couldn't work.'

The Hollywood Ten
It's possible that the Hollywood Ten would have fared better if they'd handled the HUAC hearings differently. Rather than being united over pleading their right to free speech in the First Amendment and saying nothing

Right: Made up of Hollywood figures, the Committee for the First Amendment flew to Washington in October 1947 to support the Hollywood Ten. At the bottom of the steps are Lauren Bacall and Humphrey Bogart.

Above: Despite the efforts of the Committee for the First Amendment to protect freedom of speech, when Congress cited the Ten for contempt, the studios quickly buckled under pressure from their New York financiers.

else (as once intended), their responses to the questions were evasive, verbose, disorganized and antagonistic towards the Committee.

'I think they were extremely foolish and had very bad legal advice,' said Philip Dunne, part of the Committee for the First Amendment who tried to advise the Ten. 'When you're in the lion's den, don't make the lion any madder than he is – to begin with, use the chair, in this case the First Amendment.'

On 24 November 1947, Congress voted to cite the Hollywood Ten for contempt, and three days later, the Hollywood studios announced in the 'Waldorf Statement' that the film industry would not 'knowingly employ a Communist or a member of any party or group which advocates the overthrow of the

Government of the United States by force, or by any illegal or unconstitutional method'. Philip Dunne called it 'a complete surrender to what I like to call un-Americans'.

In Los Angeles, studio heads Samuel Goldwyn, Darryl Zanuck, Harry Cohn and Dore Schary opposed the decree, but pressure from their financial backers in New York prevailed. Prompted by HUAC, Hollywood had quickly attacked itself. One didn't have to be guilty;

> Congress voted to cite the Hollywood Ten for contempt, and three days later, the Hollywood studios announced that the film industry would not 'knowingly employ a Communist'.

HANNS EISLER

ONE OF HUAC's first targets was German composer Hanns Eisler, whose entry visa in 1939 had been helped by Eleanor Roosevelt. By attacking Eisler, it was possible to besmirch both Hollywood and Eleanor Roosevelt, and thereby the 'the un-Americanism' of her husband Franklin D. Roosevelt.

A member of the Communist Party when he lived in Germany, Eisler had had his work with playwright Bertolt Brecht banned by the Nazi Party and had gone into exile. After travelling for a number of years, he made his way to Hollywood, where he worked on numerous film scores. At his HUAC hearing, one of the witnesses said: 'My purpose is to show that Mr. Eisler is the Karl Marx of communism in the musical field.' To which Eisler replied: 'I would be flattered.'

Despite no evidence being found that Eisler was plotting a Communist takeover, he was ordered to be deported from the US. In 1948, when Eisler and his wife were about to fly from New York, he read out a statement: 'I leave this country not without bitterness and infuriation. I could well understand it when in 1933 the Hitler bandits put a price on my head and drove me out. They were the evil of the period; I was proud at being driven out. But I feel heartbroken over being driven out of this beautiful country in this ridiculous way.' On his experience with HUAC he said: 'As an old anti-Fascist it became plain to me that these men represent fascism in its most direct form.' Eisler lived in Communist East Germany for the rest of his life, although he became increasingly at odds with the system.

suspicion was enough. The studios 'were frightened at the thought of boycotts of their films,' said actor Gregory Peck. 'Anything that threatened the box office threatened them; they were certainly not courageous.'

Perhaps some of the willingness for the studios to bow to the pressure of HUAC was their weakened financial status in the late 1940s, having been forced by law to sell off their cinema chains and no longer being able to dictate the length of actors' contracts. When the box office attendances also began to free fall, they'd have further cause for worry. The studios' backers might not have been sympathetic to HUAC, but with a Republican-held House and Senate from 1946, with HUAC gathering muscle and under attack financially, placating the voices in Washington at the cost of the Hollywood Ten probably seemed an easier choice.

Left: With falling box office figures and the rise of television in the late 1940s and early 1950s, Hollywood studios were perhaps more willing to sacrifice some of their best talent to appease the witch-hunt.

Although Hollywood denied that there was a blacklist, contracts were being broken by the studios using the morals cause, while those who protested at the witch-hunts quickly risked being accused themselves of being sympathetic to Communists. Coming under pressure from Warner Bros. because of his association with the Committee for the First Amendment, Humphrey Bogart placed huge advertisements in the trade papers stating that he was not, and never had been, a Communist. Even Ring Lardner Jr was fired from working on a script at Fox.

> … contracts were being broken by the studios using the morals cause, while those who protested at the witch-hunts quickly risked being accused themselves of being sympathetic to Communists.

Howard Koch also placed an advertisement denying that he'd ever been a Communist, but that he reserved the right not to say that to HUAC because it was none of their business. He called on the Hollywood community to remain firm. It did. Unfortunately not with Koch but against him, and anybody else who might be thought to have Communist sympathies. He was never told he was on the blacklist, but, as he later said, 'The telephone stopped ringing. That's all. I knew what that meant.' When some members of the Directors Guild of America proposed a motion of resistance to HUAC, they were turned upon by other members bullying them and threatening to take down their names. 'That was the most disgusting exhibition I've ever seen,' Edward Dmytryk later claimed. 'All the in-betweens were scared to death.' The motion was withdrawn.

Impact of the Blacklist

Howard Koch, one of the screenwriters of Warner Bros.' *Casablanca* (1942), was one of those named by Jack Warner at HUAC. Koch had never been a Communist but after he'd been outspoken during a strike, Warner had taken a dislike to him, and for Koch and many others, speaking up for a left-leaning union would be met with accusations of being a Communist.

Jail Sentence

Having fought the contempt citations for two and a half years through the courts, in 1950, the Hollywood Ten were denied by the Supreme Court a hearing for an appeal and were imprisoned for between six months and a year. Chained together in handcuffs and leg irons, Albert Maltz and Edward Dmytryk were sent to the prison camp at Mill Point, West Virginia. Elsewhere Ring Lardner Jr and Lester Cole found themselves in prison alongside J. Parnell Thomas, the former chair of HUAC, who was now serving a sentence for putting non-existent workers on the government payroll and claiming their salaries himself. 'It was very entertaining to see him there,' said Lardner Jr.

That year a pamphlet called *Red Channels* was published naming 151 people in film, radio and television, and questioning their loyalty as American citizens. The list included composer Leonard Bernstein, writer Dorothy Parker and actor John Garfield. Studios now consulted *Red Channels* when deciding whom to hire. 'There were hundreds and hundreds of people who had done nothing who were blacklisted,' said Dmytryk. 'They were the ones who really suffered.' When Leonard Bernstein applied to renew his passport in 1951, he had to write an affidavit of thousands of words stating that he wasn't a Communist and explaining all the well-meaning causes he'd supported before a new passport was granted.

Working under the Blacklist

Official or not, with the blacklist in place, film-makers had to find ways to cope. Before his prison sentence, Ring Lardner Jr was hired in secret to adapt a John Steinbeck story under a pseudonym. 'I had to go into a bank in Beverly Hills where Franchot Tone withdrew $10,000 in cash and gave it to me,' said Lardner Jr. Walter Bernstein was another who found himself blacklisted – from 1950 to 1958. However, he kept

> 'There were hundreds and hundreds of people who had done nothing who were blacklisted,' said director Edward Dmytryk. 'They were the ones who really suffered.'

working in television by using other writers to front his work. Fronts would put their names on the script, attend script meetings if necessary, and sometimes take a percentage of the money.

Writers could be invisible, but actors and directors couldn't hide behind fronts and pseudonyms. Actor Jeff Corey became an acting coach, while others worked more in the theatre. Paul Henreid, best known as Victor Laszlo, Ingrid Bergman's on-screen husband in *Casablanca*, had recently completed a seven-year contract with Warner Bros. when he joined the Committee for the First Amendment trip to Washington. Soon he found that he'd been blacklisted. Others on the trip hadn't, because they had studio contracts. 'The studios will look after their own, Paul', Dore Schary at MGM told him. 'You've got no one behind you.' Henreid worked less and less and in the 1950s developed a new career directing for TV. For

Right: In the comedy *The Front* (1976), which highlights how ridiculous the witch-hunts could be, Woody Allen plays an apolitical, small-time bookie and restaurant cashier who agrees to front a blacklisted friend's TV scripts. Ultimately, HUAC catches up with him.

THE FRONT

TWENTY YEARS AFTER the end of the blacklist, Walter Bernstein wrote *The Front* (1976), a film about writers and actors facing HUAC. In addition to Bernstein, its director Martin Ritt, star Zero Mostel and many of its actors had all been blacklisted.

'It is our revenge,' wrote Bernstein, but the movie treats its subject lightly, telling the story of the rise and fall of a small-time bookie and restaurant cashier, played by Woody Allen, who begins fronting the scripts of blacklisted TV writers, and soon finds himself feted as a major writing discovery.

So why did they make a comedy about such a serious topic? 'It's the only way the studio will do a picture about the blacklist,' explained Bernstein.

Joseph Losey, a move to Britain was necessary, where he directed run-of-the-mill TV shows and commercials before re-establishing himself with features. Jules Dassin successfully relocated to Europe, with his French heist drama *Rififi* (1955) becoming his best-known film.

In all, many worked less, on thinner material, and for less money than before. When Martin Ritt was first re-employed on being taken off the blacklist in 1957, he was paid $10,000 for 18 months' work. 'That's the going rate for a coffee getter,' he said. 'But I was happy to take it.' For others the consequences were graver. Not a Communist but a supporter of the Committee for the First Amendment, John Garfield was called

Below: The French crime caper *Rififi* was directed by Jules Dassin (pictured centre) after the blacklist had forced him to leave America. He was not alone. Others found work in Britain, Switzerland and Italy.

> Bartley Crum, who represented many of the Hollywood Ten, had his phones tapped and his post opened by the FBI.

twice before HUAC. For a year he wasn't offered work, and, having suffered long-term cardiac problems, in 1952 he died of a heart attack aged 39. Bartley Crum, a lawyer who represented many of the Hollywood Ten, had his phones tapped and his post opened by the FBI throughout the 1950s. Placed under surveillance, he lost most of his clients. 'Close to bankruptcy and in despair', as his daughter wrote, he informed on two colleagues who'd already been named. In 1959, he committed suicide.

Colder War

With no evidence found of subversive Communist activities, it might be thought that after the initial HUAC hearings, the fire would have run out of the witch-hunts. In fact, they became more fervent, perhaps because of the international situation. In June 1950, US troops, as part of a UN force, began fighting in the Korean War against Soviet-backed North Korea, while in 1953 Julius and Ethel Rosenberg were executed for passing information about the US atomic bomb to the Soviet Union. 'Generally the whole situation in the country was more tense,' said Lardner Jr. And with the intensification of the Cold War, HUAC began new hearings.

In 1951, actor Larry Parks, well known for portraying Al Jolson on screen, became the first Hollywood witness to admit that he'd been a Communist. When asked to name other Party members, Parks pleaded with the committee: 'You know who the people are. I don't think this is American justice, to make me choose whether to be in contempt of this Committee or crawl through the

Above: Actor Larry Parks became the first Hollywood witness to admit that he'd been a member of the Communist Party. Accepting that his movie career was over, he quickly launched a variety act.

mud for no purpose!' Nevertheless, he named names and on leaving the hearings immediately offered the cancellation of his contract at Columbia, which was accepted. Parks knew that his Hollywood career was over, and, with his wife, singer Betty Garrett, he launched a variety act, only appearing in three more films.

Co-operating with HUAC

With HUAC, you could still win favour by 'naming names' that were already known to the Committee, as writer Budd Schulberg did – naming 15. 'Frankly, I thought those people had already become so identified with the Party that I didn't feel as if I was fingering the criminals,' he said. Some felt Schulberg was missing the point. 'The problem you had to face was one of moral honour, rather than giving information,' said blacklisted writer-director Abraham Polonsky.

Below: 'It's the only thing I've ever done in my life for which I'm ashamed,' said actor Sterling Hayden of his naming names before HUAC in 1951. Although he had briefly been a member of the Communist Party, after testifying he was allowed to maintain his career.

Actor Sterling Hayden described himself as 'a romantic Communist – the only person to buy a schooner and join the Communist Party in the same week'. Although not a member for long, when he was called to appear before the Committee in 1951, he named seven names, including Abraham Polonsky 'whom I knew a bit personally and admired enormously'. The morning after he'd testified, a friend he'd named who wasn't in the movie business was fired from his job. Hayden never forgave himself and considered himself 'a rat', but he received congratulations from the right wing, including Ronald Reagan and the chairman of Paramount Pictures. 'When a man performs an act of personal betrayal of his friends, he's regarded as a 100 per cent all-American patriot,' Hayden said.

Having served his prison term, Edward Dmytryk named 26 names, telling the congressmen that he'd

> Hayden had described himself as 'the only person to buy a schooner and join the Communist Party in the same week'.

changed his attitude because of the problematic world situation. 'It wasn't enough to say "I'm no longer a member." You had to do something to prove it, otherwise you were always tarred with the same brush.' After three years without work, his career resumed apace.

Even if you weren't on the blacklist, you weren't safe, because you could be on the *grey* list. If someone hadn't been named to *Red Channels* but its staff were still unconvinced, they'd advise a studio, 'we're not sure about him, so best not to touch him'. As a result of the grey list, director Vincent Sherman didn't work for three years. When one executive admitted to Sherman why he wasn't being hired, the executive added: 'and if you tell anyone what I told you, I'll deny it.'

The Slave Rebellion

The story of the making of *Spartacus* (1960) illustrates many aspects of the blacklist. Dalton Trumbo had been one of the highest-paid screenwriters during the 1940s, but once blacklisted, he couldn't get work in California and moved his family to Mexico City. From there he managed to work under pseudonyms or fronts, on films including *Gun Crazy* and *Roman Holiday,* although the money wasn't as good. At his pre-blacklist peak, Trumbo had been earning $3000 a week at MGM, now he was being paid $2500 for a whole script.

Although by 1959, with the blacklist weakening, Trumbo could admit that he was the writer of 1956's *The Brave One,* Kirk Douglas still hired him in secret to write the screenplay for *Spartacus.* When using pseudonyms, Trumbo would pick a different one for each production to lessen the fall-out if one was traced to him, and would then be paid through a system of aliases. In this way, there would be no paper trail linking his producers to the name Dalton Trumbo. Using the name 'Sam Jackson' in all his

Right: Director Vincent Sherman felt the grey list was harder to manage than the blacklist, 'because you were fighting shadows.'

correspondence with Douglas, it was agreed that for publicity purposes, producer Edward Lewis would be named as the writer while they were setting up the film.

Crediting Trumbo

However, as the film neared release, Douglas was uncertain whom to credit as screenwriter. Edward Lewis refused to have his name on a script he hadn't written, and if they used Sam Jackson they'd have to fabricate some lies about this mysterious new writer of a major Hollywood film.

At this point the director of *Spartacus,* Stanley Kubrick, suggested they use his name, which 'horrified' Douglas and Lewis. Douglas asked Kubrick if he wouldn't be embarrassed putting his name on a script

someone else had written. 'He looked at me as if I didn't know what I was talking about. "No." He would have been delighted to take the credit.'

That night Douglas decided that he'd openly break the blacklist and credit Trumbo as the film's writer. 'All my friends told me I was being stupid, throwing my career away,' wrote Douglas in his autobiography. But for the first time in ten years, Trumbo was able to walk on to a studio lot. Douglas admitted that he wasn't trying to be a hero. 'I was just thinking, how unfair for someone to say, "Put my name on it. Let me get the credit for someone else's work."' So it seems Stanley Kubrick's ego in wanting to unfairly promote his own name inadvertently played a small role in helping end the blacklist.

> ...in 1958 an established publishing house re-issued the book, breaking the blacklist and signifying its waning.

For Trumbo, *Spartacus* was a turning point. Before it was released, producer-director Otto Preminger announced that Dalton Trumbo would be the screenwriter of his next film, *Exodus*, although it wouldn't be until the late 1970s that Trumbo would be recognized as the real Oscar-winning writer of *Roman Holiday* and *The Brave One*.

Actually, it wasn't only the making of *Spartacus* that tells us about the blacklist. The novel on which the film is based was itself a product of the blacklist. When author Howard Fast went to prison for three months for refusing to name those who'd donated to a fund for the orphans of American veterans in the Spanish Civil War, he began to write the novel *Spartacus*, a story of a thwarted slave rebellion against the Roman Republic. But as publishing was also subject to the blacklist, Fast was forced to self-publish the book in 1951. It was a hit and in 1958 an established publishing house re-issued the book, breaking the blacklist and signifying its waning. The following year, Douglas bought the film rights.

Left: *Spartacus* was a product of the blacklist: it is based on a novel written by a blacklisted writer, was adapted by a blacklisted screenwriter and it tells the story of a rebellion against oppression.

THIS MAN LIVED BY THE JUNGLE LAW OF THE DOCKS!

COLUMBIA PICTURES presents

MARLON BRANDO

ON THE WATERFRONT

AN ELIA KAZAN PRODUCTION

co-starring KARL MALDEN · LEE J. COBB

with ROD STEIGER · PAT HENNING and introducing EVA MARIE SAINT

Produced by SAM SPIEGEL   Screen Play by BUDD SCHULBERG   Music by LEONARD BERNSTEIN   Directed by ELIA KAZAN

Above: Many regard *On The Waterfront* (1954), in which a New York longshoreman testifies against his corrupt union, as screenwriter Budd Schulberg's and director Elia Kazan's defence for having named names to HUAC.

On the film's release, the American Legion, the world's largest veterans' organization, sent a letter to its 17,000 members telling them not to see it because of Trumbo's involvement, while Hedda Hopper wrote in her *LA Times* column that *Spartacus* 'was sold to Universal from a book written by a Commie and the screen script was written by a Commie, so don't go see it'. The film, however, was a box office hit. Today *Spartacus* is considered a classic; the phrase, 'I'm Spartacus', is shorthand for solidarity and for not denouncing others in defiance of corrupt authority, just as the Hollywood Ten had stood firm against HUAC and not named names.

> 'I'm Spartacus', is now shorthand for solidarity and for not denouncing others in defiance of corrupt authority.

On The Waterfront

If *Spartacus* is an example of the blacklist, what about a film from those who named names? When director Elia Kazan was called to testify before the House Committee, he was highly successful on both Broadway

Right: Senator Joseph McCarthy in 1953. Although he is the name most closely associated with the witch-hunts, McCarthy wasn't directly involved in investigating Hollywood. His bullying and unsubstantiated claims ultimately undermined his efforts and discredited the blacklist.

SINATRA EXECUTES PRIVATE SLOVIK

IN 1960, FRANK Sinatra announced that he'd hired blacklisted Albert Maltz to write a screenplay for *The Execution of Private Slovik* (the true story of an American soldier executed in World War II for desertion – the only such case since the Civil War). The Hearst press attacked Sinatra for hiring Maltz, as did the American Legion, and disc jockeys were pressed not to play his records. At the time, Sinatra was supporting John F. Kennedy's election campaign and Sinatra (pictured, below right, with Kennedy) soon found himself under pressure from the campaign manager. Feeling the heat, he quickly had second thoughts about hiring a blacklisted writer, fired Maltz and sold on the rights to the book.

and in Hollywood, having directed Arthur Miller's *Death of a Salesman* on stage as well as both the stage and screen versions of Tennessee Williams's *A Streetcar Named Desire* (1951). Kazan appeared twice before the Committee in 1952, supplying it with the names of eight former members of the Group Theater and other Party members. All the names were already known to the Committee.

In naming names, Kazan destroyed many of his friendships, including that with Arthur Miller. His excuse was that he'd resigned from the Communist Party in the 1930s when it put him on trial for not following its instructions in how he ran the apolitical Group Theater. But, of course, in testifying, he also managed to keep his successful career going, making major movies throughout the blacklist and beyond.

One of them was *On The Waterfront* (1954), on which he worked with screenwriter Budd Schulberg. The film, loosely based on fact, tells the story of a New York longshoreman, played by Marlon Brando, who witnesses the corruption of his union and risks his life in testifying against it at a Crime Commission. Many regard the film as Schulberg and Kazan's defence for co-operating with HUAC. The film was a commercial and critical hit, winning eight Oscars, including those for Brando, Schulberg, Kazan and producer Sam Spiegel.

Kazan went on to other successes with films such as *East of Eden* and *Splendor in the Grass,* but many in Hollywood never forgave him. When he was honoured at the 1998 Academy Awards, many of the members of the Academy refused to give him a standing ovation.

End of the Blacklist
In 1954, Republican Senator Joseph McCarthy, who, although he didn't investigate Hollywood, is the man most associated with the anti-Communist witch-hunts, was censured by the Senate. His

> Loosely based on fact, *On The Waterfront* tells the story of a New York longshoreman who witnesses the corruption of his union and risks his life in testifying against it.

tirades, bullying and unsubstantiated claims about Communists working in the Government had begun to win him more enemies than friends both in Washington and the country as a whole. It was the beginning of the end for McCarthy, but although the hearings stopped, the black and grey lists were still in place. It wasn't until 1965 that Ring Lardner Jr received his first credit after the blacklist with *The Cincinnati Kid* and that Abraham Polonsky could begin to work openly again. But Lionel Stander was still blacklisted.

> Hollywood films have in the main always been politically conservative or simply escapist. If a few films addressing contemporary issues were made in the 1930s and 1940s, fewer were shot once the fear of the blacklist was in place.

So, were any of their movies made prior to the blacklist subversive? Hollywood films have in the main always been politically conservative or simply escapist. If a few films addressing contemporary issues were made in the 1930s and 1940s, fewer were shot once the fear of the blacklist was in place, either because the film-makers who might make them weren't able to work or because others weren't prepared to risk doing anything that could be interpreted as subversive.

And did HUAC achieve anything? According to Philip Dunne, it never found any evidence that wasn't already known to the Los Angeles Police Department and the FBI, who had moles in the Hollywood Communist Party and therefore knew exactly who the Communists were. HUAC's activities might have taken the more left-leaning edge out of the unions and snuffed out some of the criticism of American foreign policy, but it also left a great deal of bitterness that lasted for the rest of the lives of those concerned.

Many believe that anti-Communism was an obsession that was more likely to destroy democracy in the USA than Communism itself – HUAC overriding the First and Fifth Amendments in the

Above: Screenwriter Carl Foreman with Winston Churchill in 1964. Blacklisted, Foreman moved to Britain in the early 1950s, where he co-wrote, uncredited, *The Bridge on the River Kwai*.

> A member of the Hollywood community could denounce a friend for having uttered a slight criticism of capitalism.

name of American democracy. While HUAC was rooting out Communism in the USA, the climate it created shared something with the Eastern Bloc totalitarian regimes it feared; and while Stalin's show trials of political prisoners made a mockery of the proclaimed fairness of the Communist system, HUAC itself was unconstitutional. An unguarded word to one's next-door neighbour against the Party in Russia could result in people losing their jobs, just as a member of the Hollywood community could denounce a friend for having uttered a slight criticism of capitalism. In Russia, an informer might receive a better apartment; in Hollywood the informer could be crossed off the blacklist and go back to work. As fellow Republican Senator Ralph E. Flanders said of Joseph McCarthy: 'Were the Junior Senator from Wisconsin [McCarthy] in the pay of the Communists, he could not have done a better job for them.'

POLAND'S HIGH NOON

A FORMER MEMBER of the Communist Party, Carl Foreman was called to testify while he was writing the screenplay for *High Noon* (1952), the story of an honest Western marshal who returns to defend his town against criminals but finds all the other townsfolk too cowardly to take a stand with him. Facing the Committee, Foreman refused to name names, was blacklisted and before the film was released he moved to Britain, where he worked for the rest of his life. The public, of course, just enjoyed a good story and *High Noon* went on to be regarded worldwide as a classic Western.

In 1989, an image from *High Noon* was used for the Polish Solidarity Party's election campaign – the first free elections held in Communist Poland. The blacklisted had been accused of inserting Communist propaganda into their films, but Foreman's film was now being held up as a symbol of justice and used *against* Communism. The Solidarity Party went on to win almost all the seats eligible to them and were given a voice in the government. By the end of the year, Poland's prime minister was a member of Solidarity.

THE MOB

**Al Capone only spent 24 hours in Los Angeles in 1927 before being escorted
from the city, but in that time he managed to visit a movie studio and comment:
'That's a grand racket.' As Hollywood grew during the 1930s, its wealth
drew New York and Chicago mobsters west. They extorted the studios, befriended
some of the actors and slept with the starlets. And Hollywood also
enabled their influence to reach as high as Washington.**

◆

'Don't ever think Hollywood is some friggin' Disneyland.'

After Prohibition ended in 1933, and with Hollywood becoming more established, the Chicago and New York Mobs looked to the studios as a new area to be exploited. Understanding that you can't make movies without film to put in the cameras, the Mob made sure that they were on the payroll of the Dupont Film Corporation; which supplied film stock to the studios.

**Mobster Johnny Rosselli had a varied career. Starting out in the
Chicago of Al Capone he went on to extorting movie studios,
working as a Hollywood producer, developing Las Vegas casinos and
even testifying at the US Senate about an alleged 1961 CIA plot to
assassinate Fidel Castro.**

And when in 1933 the studios faced a strike by actors and technicians over a 50 per cent pay cut, it was mobster Johnny Rosselli to whom Nicholas Schenck, who managed a chain of cinemas and the MGM studio, turned for help. As scab workers were hired by the moguls to break the picket lines, Rosselli brought in outside muscle to hit any picketer who tried to stop them. The police, meanwhile, had been bought off, and within a week the technicians' union – the International Association of Theatrical and Stage Employees (IATSE) – gave up their strike, leaving the producers able to force an open shop. After that, Rosselli was put on MGM's payroll.

Willie Bioff

On the surface the powerful IATSE might have been representing the interests of its members, but it had been infiltrated at the top by the Mob, whose own

Above: While the studios were keeping mobsters on the payroll, they were also mixing with politicians. Here MGM's Nicholas Schenck (centre) looks on as lawyer Basil O'Connor presents a cheque to President Franklin D. Roosevelt.

> With the threat of shutting down projectionists across the country, Bioff and Browne took kickbacks, each receiving $50,000.

interests came first. Thus, working through IATSE, Willie Bioff came to extort millions from the studios, in a criminal career that had begun in Chicago in the mid-1920s when he lured Illinois country girls into the big city and prostitution.

The Depression ruined his brothel business, so he began a protection racket on Chicago shops where he became aware of George E. Browne: while Bioff would be taking money off the Jewish shops, Browne would be targeting the Gentile establishments. Natural

partners, they joined forces, aimed higher and settled on Chicago's cinemas, offering a 'no strike guarantee' from the projectionists' union in return for kickbacks. Winning the approval of the Mob, Browne took over as president of IATSE, with Bioff as his enforcer. In Hollywood, Browne and Bioff worked a similar scam. With the threat of shutting down projectionists across the country, they took kickbacks from the studios, each receiving $50,000 from the major studios, and, in return, only pushing for small improvements for their union members. Louis B. Mayer and other moguls estimated that they'd saved about $15 million by buying off Bioff and Browne.

HOT TODDY

ALTHOUGH THE CIRCUMSTANCES remain a mystery, the death of actress Thelma Todd could be an example of what can happen in Hollywood if you fall in and then out with bad company. From 1926, Todd acted in comedies alongside Laurel & Hardy and Buster Keaton. Then in 1932, she married former bootlegger Pasquale DiCicco, right-hand man in LA to mobster Lucky Luciano, head of the New York Genovese Family. Their marriage turned violent and she divorced him in 1934 when she began a relationship with director Roland West, with whom she opened a roadhouse on the coast – Thelma Todd's Sidewalk Café. Luciano, who'd also been one of her lovers,

wanted to start a private, and illegal, gambling room at the Sidewalk, but Todd resisted. With Luciano trying to muscle in on the Sidewalk, Todd sought help and contacted district attorney Buron Fitts. Her meeting with Fitts was scheduled for Tuesday 18 December 1935, but she didn't live long enough to make her appointment.

Three days earlier, on Saturday 15 December, Todd had attended an LA party, where she was seen merrily drunk, despite encountering ex-husband DiCicco there and having a brief argument. In the small hours, her chauffeur dropped her off at home. Then on the Monday morning her maid found her body slumped over the steering wheel of her car in her garage.

The coroner's verdict classed her death as accidental from carbon monoxide poisoning, but this didn't take into account her missing teeth, her broken nose, fractured ribs and her blood-splattered dress. One explanation offered was that in her death throes she'd had a spasm and banged her head against the steering wheel. Well, that's possible …

The scheduled meeting with DA Fitts wasn't in Luciano's interest, but nor, in fact, was it in Fitts's, because he was connected to the Mob. Thelma Todd's friends claimed that she hadn't seemed suicidal, so, was she really so drunk that she'd climbed into her car, turned the engine on and then fallen asleep? And would a spasm be sufficient to fracture her ribs and knock out some teeth? Or was it possible that a broken-hearted DiCicco killed her? Or had she crossed two of LA's most powerful establishments: the Mob and the corrupt legal system? The mystery remains unsolved.

Another mobster was Benjamin 'Bugsy' Siegel; he moved from New York to Los Angeles in the late 1930s to muscle in on the existing gambling rackets, while getting kickbacks from the studios. 'Suppose on your next picture,' he said to the studios, 'the script has been finished, the director is ready to go, the stars are ready, the stagehands, everybody is drawing a salary, and when you shout "Action!" the extras walk out.' The studios understood Siegel's hold over the Screen Extras Guild and paid him off: it's estimated that Siegel was receiving at least $500,000 a year from them.

The two worlds of the Mafia and Hollywood mixed socially, too. Although he had a wife and family, Siegel, a friend of George Raft's from his New York

Above: The wreckage after Willie Bioff was killed in a car bomb at his house in Phoenix, Arizona, in 1955. Bioff had been sent to prison in 1941 for running an extortion scam with the studios. Two years later, he had entered the witness protection programme.

days, began going out with bit-part player and Mafia girl Virginia Hill, while Johnny Rosselli had affairs with actresses Donna Reid, Lana Turner and Betty Hutton. Mickey Cohen socialized with Dean Martin, Jerry Lewis and Robert Mitchum, and Jean Harlow had a relationship with mobster Abner 'Longy' Zwillman, who gave Harry Cohn the $500,000 he needed in 1932 to buy out his partner Joe Brandt at Columbia Pictures.

When the racketeering trial began in 1943, Bioff and Browne vanished into the witness protection programme.

Although a union man, Willie Bioff made no effort to disguise his new wealth in Hollywood. He bought a ranch in the San Fernando Valley, built a house with a pool, filled his home with antiques, and flashed around his gold and diamond business cards. Eventually the law caught up with him, and in 1941 he and Browne were given 20-year sentences for tax irregularities and union pay-offs. In the same case, Joseph Schenck, Nicholas Schenck's brother and chairman of the board of 20th Century Fox, who'd been Bioff and Browne's contact in the studio, was sentenced to five years for his involvement – though he only served 12 months before being released with a full presidential pardon. He'd earlier contributed $500,000 towards Harry S. Truman's campaign and now Truman was President.

When Bioff went to prison, his Mob associate Nicholas Deani Circella went on the run. With the Chicago Outfit nervous that Bioff or others might talk about their involvement, it's believed that a hit was put on Circella's girlfriend, Estelle Carey. She was attacked at home, stabbed with an ice pick and a broken whiskey bottle, before being tied to a dining chair, doused in petrol and set on fire.

If it was a Mafia hit, the murder of Estelle Carey was the first known Mafia hit on a woman in America. If it was intended to silence Bioff, it had the opposite effect. Appalled by the murder, Bioff agreed to talk and named many Mob connections, including Frank Nitti, who fronted the Chicago Outfit. When the indictments were handed out, Nitti, who'd already served 18 months in prison with Al Capone for tax evasion, shot himself.

When the racketeering trial began in 1943, Bioff and Browne vanished into the witness protection programme. (Working in casinos, Bioff was killed by a car bomb outside his home in Phoenix, Arizona, in 1955). The Chicago mobsters involved and Johnny Rosselli were found guilty and sentenced to ten years each. However, all were paroled in August 1947, having served less than three years, without the parole board even seeing the notes on the cases. Through bribes, the Mob had managed to buy influence with lawyers and politicians and also pay off the $200,000 in taxes and fines that were due.

One crucial link was Paul Dillon, a lawyer connected to the Mob, who'd also been Harry Truman's campaign manager during his first attempt to reach the Senate in 1934. One legislator asked if the parole board had taken $500,000 in return for the gangsters' freedom. The charge wasn't denied.

Mafia Movies

On his release from prison, Johnny Rosselli began working directly for Hollywood with a job at Eagle-Lion Studios where Joe Schenck's nephew was a producer. Ironically, one of Eagle-Lion's best films was *T-Men* (1947), a story about a group of Treasury agents investigating a counterfeiting ring.

Left: Johnny Rosselli may have been sentenced to ten years in prison, but within three years he was released and back in Hollywood. Moving up from extorting the studios, he now worked as a producer of B-pictures, including the very successful *T-Men*.

Left: Mobster Aniello 'Neil' Dellacroce, who later became an underboss of the Gambino crime family, with Frank Sinatra in 1950. Sinatra's life would be tainted by his connections to some of the most infamous mob families.

In 1950 Rosselli testified to the Kefauver Committee investigating interstate organized crime. Rosselli admitted to Senator Kefauver that he knew nearly all the Mafia leaders throughout the country, which led Kefauver to declare the Capone syndicate a national organization, the first time such an accusation had been made.

After the Kefauver hearings, Rosselli had trouble finding work in Hollywood and moved to represent the Chicago Mob developing the casinos in Las Vegas, but not before using his Mob influence to revive the career of a fading singer and actor – Frank Sinatra.

Frank Sinatra

Rumours of Frank Sinatra's links with the Mafia shadowed him throughout his life. According to released FBI files, they concluded that he was neither a member of the Mafia nor had business relations with them, but he couldn't deny knowing Mafia members socially.

On 22 December 1946, the senior members of the American Mafia families held a conference in Havana, Cuba. This was chaired by Lucky Luciano, who'd been exiled from the US, and Meyer Lansky, head of the Jewish Syndicate, and included representatives from all the major syndicates in organized crime. Sinatra, it's said, provided the entertainment. Some even say he flew down to Cuba with Luciano's cousin. It's also alleged that he gave Luciano a gold cigarette case with the inscription: 'To my dear pal Charlie from his friend Frank.'

Then, years later in 1962, Sinatra, along with Dean Martin, Sammy Davis Jr and Eddie Fisher, gave a concert at the Villa Venice Supper Club in Wheeling, Illinois. Why did they perform in such a small place when they could play Vegas? Because, the FBI believed, the Villa Venice was owned by Mafia boss Sam Giancana.

It would seem to be an association Sinatra could enjoy: he provided the Mafia with glamour and legitimacy, and they offered him at the very least a little toughness in the public eye, if not actual muscle. Sinatra had always fancied himself as a tough guy, but if he began a fight he'd most likely let one of his minders finish it for him. With Mob connections, he had some edge.

> Sinatra provided the Mafia with glamour and legitimacy, and they offered him at the very least a little toughness in the public eye, if not actual muscle.

From Here to Eternity

When it came to casting the film *From Here to Eternity* in 1952, Sinatra's name wouldn't have been high up the list. At that time, he'd appeared in 12 movies but definitely wasn't a movie star, his singing career was on the slide and he'd been dropped by Columbia Records. When it was suggested to Columbia Pictures' head Harry Cohn that Sinatra be given a supporting role in *From Here to Eternity,* Cohn responded: 'Who the hell wants to see that skinny asshole in a major movie?'

HOLLYWOOD NITE LIFE

IN 1945, MICKEY Cohen involved Frank Sinatra in investing in *Hollywood Nite Life,* a weekly entertainment newspaper. Run by Jimmy Tarantino, the magazine would dig up dirt on Hollywood celebrities and then threaten to publish the information if the stars didn't pay them off. According to Tarantino, Sinatra put up $15,000 to launch the magazine. Ultimately, the stars had had enough and brought Tarantino to trial. He was convicted for extortion.

Above: Frank Sinatra with Donna Reed in *From Here to Eternity* (1952). With Sinatra's music and movie careers having stalled, it was rumoured that Johnny Rosselli put Mob pressure on Harry Cohn of Columbia Pictures to cast Sinatra in the movie.

Sinatra signed to Capitol Records, recorded the songs for which he's best known, and became a far bigger star than before.

But, the story goes, Johnny Rosselli threatened Cohn with the consequences if Sinatra wasn't given the part. Sinatra was subsequently offered the role and it won him a Best Supporting Actor Oscar. His film career was re-launched, he signed to Capitol Records, recorded the songs for which he's best known, and became a far bigger star than he'd been before.

Lana Turner and Johnny Stompanato

Lana Turner married eight times and was known for having many lovers, but when she found herself in bed with the Mafia it led to a fatal stabbing and a scandal that dogged her for the rest of her life.

In 1957, Turner's fourth marriage to Lex Barker, an actor who played Tarzan, ended. According to Cheryl Crane, Turner's teenage daughter from her second marriage, Turner threw Barker out after Cheryl revealed that Barker had been molesting her for years.

SAMMY DAVIS JR

BEST KNOWN FOR her role as Hitchcock's icy blonde in *Vertigo* (1958), Kim Novak was under contract to Columbia when, in 1957, she began a relationship with Sammy Davis Jr. Anticipating the reactions of some to an inter-racial relationship, they tried to keep their affair quiet. When Harry Cohn heard about them, he was appalled. 'What's with this nigger? If he doesn't straighten up he'll be minus another eye.' Three years earlier, Davis had lost his left eye in a car crash.

Cohn had words with Johnny Rosselli and a gunman visited Davis backstage in Vegas, telling him that he'd be killed if he continued the affair. Davis was defiant. So Mob-connected Hollywood lawyer Sidney Korshak explained to him that he'd never

work again, before confronting Novak with private sex films that Davis had made of his other well-known lovers. Dissuaded one way or another, Novak and Davis ended their relationship.

That, however, wasn't the end of problems for Davis. In 1960 he was ready to marry Swede May Britt (pictured with Davis) when, it was rumoured, John F. Kennedy persuaded him to delay the wedding until after the presidential election. (At that time, inter-racial marriages were still against the law in 31 US states.) Then, in January 1961, Joseph P. Kennedy, JFK's father, banned Davis from attending a gala arranged by Sinatra on the eve of Kennedy's inauguration.

> Rumours spread that Turner's on-screen romance with a young, pre-James Bond, Sean Connery was being continued off-screen.

Turner then met Johnny Stompanato, who worked for Mickey Cohen – although she said she didn't realize his Mob connections at the time. When she did find out, she was already involved with him and did try to distance herself, but he was violent and not easily deterred.

While she was filming *Another Time, Another Place* in England in 1957, rumours spread that her on-screen romance with a young, pre-James Bond, Sean Connery was being continued off-screen. Word reached Stompanato, who flew to London. Turner managed to keep him away from the set and cooped up in her

London home, but one day, Stompanato, consumed with jealousy, burst into the studios and waved a gun at Connery, warning him to stay away from his girlfriend. Connery wrestled the gun off him and knocked Stompanato out.

The following spring Turner was nominated for an Oscar for her role in *Peyton Place*, but she couldn't face bringing Stompanato to the awards ceremony and instead took 14-year-old Cheryl, leaving Stompanato at home, watching the Oscars on TV, drinking. When Turner returned after an Oscar party, Stompanato gave

Below: Sean Connery and Lana Turner filming *Another Time, Another Place* in England in 1957. When Turner's boyfriend Johnny Stompanato, waving a gun, confronted Connery and Turner over an alleged affair, Connery knocked him out.

her a beating, but in a professional way, she would later claim, where the bruises could be covered up. 'He yanked me up and began hitting me with his fists,' she wrote in her autobiography. 'I went flying across the room into the bar, sending glasses shattering to the floor.' Still, they went to bed together and a few days later moved to a grander house. 'Underlying everything was my shame,' Turner wrote. 'I didn't want anybody to know … how foolish I'd been, how I'd taken him at face value and had been completely duped.'

A month after the Oscars, Stompanato was found dead at home from a knife wound and the only witnesses were Cheryl and Turner. According to mother and daughter, Turner and Stompanato were having a furious fight in their bedroom, with Stompanato screaming that Turner was going to die. Hearing the commotion, Cheryl

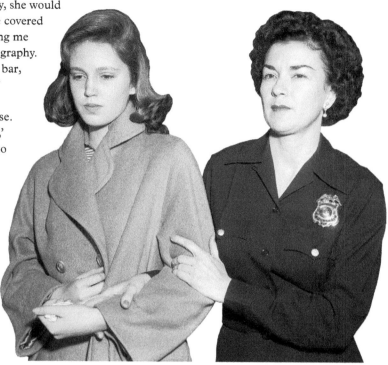

Above: In April 1958, Lana Turner's 14-year-old daughter, Cheryl Crane, claimed that she'd hurried into her mother's bedroom holding a kitchen knife and that Stompanato had run on to the blade.

> One theory is that Lana Turner stabbed Stompanato in the bed that they shared as, tellingly, by the time the police arrived the bedding had been removed.

picked up a 10-inch carving knife (bought by her mother that day) and rushed to intervene. Stompanato ran into the knife and bled to death. According to Turner, his final words were: 'Cheryl, what have you done?'

Rather than calling the police or an ambulance, Turner first rang her lawyer Jerry Giesler, who hurried over, followed by her publicist. Cheryl called her father. Only two hours later did Giesler telephone the police. When they arrived, the body had been moved and there was very little blood on it, with only smudged fingerprints on the knife. Giesler, although not present at the time of death, helped Turner and Cheryl tell their story.

Mickey Cohen and others in Hollywood didn't believe that Cheryl was strong enough to kill Stompanato, who could stand up for himself. 'I think he was in bed by himself, sleeping,' said Cohen. 'Only way Cheryl or someone else could have done it is if he was asleep …'. One theory is that Lana Turner stabbed Stompanato in the bed that they shared as, tellingly, by the time the police arrived, the bedding had been removed. Giesler, many years later, was allegedly quoted as saying that the bed 'looked like a hog had been butchered in it', which it wouldn't have done if Stompanato had been stabbed standing up and fallen to the floor.

Giesler successfully argued that Cheryl was too traumatized to testify, leaving Turner the only witness to the incident to take the witness stand. A majority verdict found Stompanato's death the result of justifiable homicide and Cheryl was released. 'It's the first time in my life I've ever seen a dead man convicted of his own murder,' Mickey Cohen said.

Above: Lana Turner was the only witness to take the stand at her daughter's trial. Stompanato's death was deemed a 'justifiable homicide' and Cheryl was released. Later, Turner settled out of court in a civil suit brought by Stompanato's family.

After Stompanato's death put Turner back in the headlines, *Peyton Place* received a 32 per cent box office boost, going on to become the second highest-grossing film of 1958. Mickey Cohen, meanwhile, helped Stompanato's family bring a civil suit stating that Turner herself had killed Stompanato. The case was settled out of court for $20,000. Cohen kept himself in business, too. Shortly after Stompanato's death, he sold some Turner–Stompanato love letters to the Press.

While filming that year, Connery was staying at the Hollywood Roosevelt Hotel when he received a menacing call from one of Mickey Cohen's associates. 'Get out of town or a contract will be put on your life,' was the message. On the advice of the studio, Connery moved to a small guesthouse outside Los Angeles for the rest of the shoot.

> While filming in Hollywood that year, Connery received a menacing call: 'Get out of town or a contract will be put on your life.'

Politics and the Mafia

Frank Sinatra's connections with the Mafia moved up a gear when Senator John F. Kennedy ran for President. In December 1959, Kennedy's father, Joseph P. Kennedy, invited Sinatra to the family home in Massachusetts to encourage him to support his son's bid as the Democrat candidate for the presidency. However, according to Sinatra's daughter Tina, more

Right: Frank Sinatra campaigning with John F. Kennedy in 1960. That February Sinatra introduced Kennedy to Judith Exner, with whom the politician began a long affair. In March, Sinatra also introduced her to mobster Sam Giancana, and they too began a relationship.

Below: Sinatra with fellow member of the Rat Pack, Peter Lawford and Bobby Kennedy in July 1961. When JFK became President and Bobby Kennedy began investigating Sam Giancana, Sinatra's Mob connections meant that he was kept at arm's length by the White House.

specifically, Joseph Kennedy asked Sinatra for help delivering the union vote in the 1960 West Virginia and Illinois primaries, 'because [Kennedy] knew Dad had access to Sam Giancana'.

Kennedy wouldn't have been the favourite Democrat candidate in Illinois, because his brother Bobby Kennedy, as chief counsel of the 1957–9 Senate

> The Mafia, they believe, helped put Kennedy in the White House. And Sinatra had played his role.

Labor Rackets Committee, had been trying to clean up the unions controlled by the Chicago Mob. But according to Tina Sinatra, Giancana agreed to the favour, telling her father: 'It's a couple of phone calls.' Kennedy won those primaries and later that year won a very close election. Journalist Seymour Hersch, among others, now says 'Sam delivered the election'. The Mafia, they believe, helped put Kennedy in the White House. And Sinatra had played his role.

Apart from politics, Sinatra would also be involved in Kennedy's busy love life. In February 1960, during the presidential campaign, Kennedy stopped in Las Vegas, where Sinatra was filming *Ocean's 11*. At the Rat Pack's Sands Casino show, Sinatra introduced Kennedy to 27-year-old Judith Exner, and the following day Kennedy invited her for lunch at the private patio of Sinatra's suite. Exner, unlike Kennedy's many one-night stands, would later begin a relationship that lasted more than 18 months.

The following month, at the Fontainebleau Hotel in Miami, Sinatra also introduced Exner to Sam Giancana and she began a relationship with him, too. According to crime writer Douglas Thompson, Sinatra was responsible for 'planting Judith Exner on Kennedy on behalf of the Mafia'. Exner admitted that at first perhaps Giancana was using her to reach Kennedy, but, she said, 'it became more than that.' She also became friends with Johnny Rosselli.

Old Blue Eyes Sees Red

When Peter Lawford, who was married to Kennedy's sister Pat, asked if the President could stay at Sinatra's Palm Springs home during a West Coast fundraiser in 1962, Sinatra leapt into action. Sinatra had previously been kept at arm's length, only ever going to the White House twice, both times when Jackie Kennedy was away (she couldn't stand him), and always entering by the side door. He even had a helipad built and extra phone lines installed for the President.

However, with brother Bobby Kennedy, now Attorney General, investigating Sam Giancana, and the President made aware by the FBI how closely Judith Exner and Sinatra brought him to Giancana and Johnny Rosselli, he had to distance himself from the singer. When Sinatra heard Kennedy wasn't going to visit him after all, he was livid. 'He called Bobby every name in the book,' said Lawford. George Jacobs, Sinatra's valet, remembered how Sinatra went outside with a sledgehammer and began hacking into the concrete helipad. Kennedy, meanwhile, went to stay at Bing Crosby's Palm Spring house instead. After that, Lawford was frozen out of Sinatra's Rat Pack. In fact, Sinatra even chose Bing Crosby to replace Lawford in their next film, *Robin and the 7 Hoods* (1964).

> Sinatra introduced Kennedy to Judith Exner and shortly after to Sam Giancana. She began relationships with both of them.

In 1960, Sinatra had bought into the Cal Neva lodge and casino, which straddles the border between California and Nevada, but in the summer of 1963, his relationship with the Mafia tipped in his disfavour. A story reached the newspapers that San Giancana had been staying at Cal Neva, although Giancana was one of 11 gangsters banned by Nevada's Gaming Control Board from even setting foot in a Nevada casino. Sinatra was called before the board's chairman, but under questioning began arguing and lost any chance he'd have of keeping his gambling licence. Although he maintained his interest in politics and campaigning, Sinatra's Mafia connections had spoilt his relationship with the Kennedys.

The Godfather

Even if it wasn't true that the Mafia had used their leverage to win Sinatra his role in *From Here to Eternity*, the story wasn't going to be forgotten. By the late 1960s, Mario Puzo was the author of a few respected but poor-selling novels, had a large family and was broke with a $20,000 gambling debt. So, he decided

PARAMOUNT PICTURES PRESENTS

The Godfather

to write something commercial and came up with the novel *The Godfather*. Paramount Pictures optioned the book, but as recent films about the Mob had failed they wanted an Italian-American director so that the audience would 'be able to smell the spaghetti'. After top directors turned the project down, Italian-American Francis Ford Coppola was offered the job. He was in a similar position to Puzo: his earlier films were respected but hadn't earned him much money, he was broke and this looked like a money-spinner. So, he signed up.

> Invited to read *The Godfather* script, mobster Joe Colombo didn't get beyond the first page before he made clear what concerned him most: he wanted the word 'Mafia' removed from the film.

The Mafia, however, let it be known that they didn't want the film made. The Los Angeles Police Department warned the film's producer Al Ruddy that he was being followed. He swapped cars with his assistant Bettye McCartt and one night she heard gunfire outside her house – Ruddy's car had been shot up and a note left on the dashboard telling him to shut down the film. In addition, the offices of Paramount's parent company Gulf & Western had to be evacuated twice because of bomb threats.

It was clearly time to talk, so mobster Joe Colombo went to Al Ruddy, who assured him the film wouldn't demean the Italian-American community. Invited to read the script, Colombo didn't get beyond the first page before he made clear what concerned him most: he wanted the word 'Mafia' removed from the film. In fact, it only appeared once in the script anyway and the change was easily made.

Persuaded that they weren't being unfairly portrayed, the Mafia now supported the film.

Left: The Mob had menaced the production of *The Godfather*, but on learning that they weren't, in their eyes, being unfairly portrayed, they began to support the movie. The film-makers suddenly found New York's previously obstructive Teamsters very co-operative.

ROSEMARY'S BABY

FRANK SINATRA WAS known for only doing two takes of a shot before he'd insist on moving on. If that wasn't enough for the director, that was the director's problem. But in 1968, Sinatra's young wife Mia Farrow – at 23 she was 30 years his junior – was cast as the lead in *Rosemary's Baby*, and, to draw out the performance he wanted, the film's director, Roman Polanski, was prepared to shoot 30 takes if necessary. Farrow didn't complain but Peter Bart, the Paramount executive overseeing the production, was soon paid a visit by a Sinatra consigliere, who urged Bart to tell Polanski to limit the number of takes to under three, and, in return, his legs wouldn't be broken. Unperturbed, Bart didn't deliver the message – he knew that Polanski would ignore it – and his legs remained unbroken, while the film went on to be a big hit and Farrow was nominated for a Golden Globe Award.

Around that time, however, Bart did stop taking notes about his experiences in the movie industry. He had come to Paramount having been a reporter on the *New York Times* and had reassured himself that, should he lose his new job in the movie business, if he'd kept careful notes he could at least write a revealing book on the workings of a Hollywood studio. His experience with Sinatra hadn't rattled him, but a conversation with Mob-connected Hollywood lawyer Sidney Korshak made him rethink his note-taking.

Korshak, known as the best fixer in the business, asked Bart one day at the studio: 'Peter, do you know the best insurance policy in the world that absolutely guarantees continued breathing?' Bart shook his head. 'It's silence,' said Korshak, peering at Bart. Taking on board the wisdom of Korshak's words, Bart not only ceased keeping a private record of his observations, but went home and burnt all his existing notes.

Puzo only included rumours about the Mob's involvement in casting Sinatra in *From Here to Eternity*, but life might have imitated art in the casting of Al Martino in *The Godfather*.

Having until that point found the city of New York obstructive in filming *The Godfather*, now, according to Paramount's head of production Robert Evans, 'New York finally opened up like a World's Fair – on our side were the garbagemen, the longshoremen, the Teamsters …'.

No Horse's Head

In *The Godfather*, Puzo included this thinly veiled repetition of the rumours about Sinatra's casting in *From Here to Eternity*: when a Hollywood studio doesn't want to cast Johnny Fontane, an Italian-American crooner whose career is fading, Fontane's Mob connections put a horse's head in the studio chief's bed and he quickly changes his mind.

It was fiction, but life might have imitated art in the casting of Al Martino in the Johnny Fontane role. A few years after Martino became a star in the early 1950s with his worldwide hit 'Here In My Heart', his management company was taken over by a Mafia-connected organization. Worried by this and ordered to pay a $75,000 upfront fee, Martino moved to England for a while, and though by the time of *The Godfather*, he was back in the US, working in Las Vegas, his career was past its best.

Then Phyllis McGuire, Sam Giancana's girlfriend, read *The Godfather*. 'Al,' she said to Martino. 'Johnny Fontane is you, and I know you can play it in the movie.' Martino, who'd never acted before, approached Paramount, but, understandably, they weren't interested in casting him. So, Martino used his own connections.

Left: Al Martino (left) with Marlon Brando in *The Godfather*. Unwanted for the role, Martino said he had to use his own Mob connections to be cast. 'There was no horse's head,' he commented, 'but I had ammunition…I went to my godfather.'

'Coppola didn't want me,' Martino said. 'There was no horse's head, but I had ammunition ... I had to step on some toes to get people to realize that I was in the effing movie. I went to my godfather, [Mafia boss] Russ Bufalino.'

End of an Era

By the mid-1970s, the Mob generation that had influenced Hollywood from the 1940s was dying off, although not necessarily as they might have hoped. In the summer of 1976, Johnny Rosselli talked to a Special Intelligence Committee (SIC) investigating the excesses of the CIA and told them how he and Sam Giancana had been recruited by the CIA in a plan to assassinate Fidel Castro. A few months later, Giancana was shot dead at home in Illinois. He, too, had been due to testify before the SIC about the CIA's collusion with the Mafia to kill President Kennedy. Then a year later Rosselli was choked to death, his legs sawn off, and his body sealed in a 55-gallon oil drum before being dumped off the Florida Gold Coast. His end might never have been known if gases escaping from his decomposing body hadn't made the barrel bob to the surface.

In 1977, Johnny Rosselli was choked to death and his body sealed in a 55-gallon oil drum. His end might never have been known if gases escaping from his decomposing body hadn't made the barrel bob to the surface.

Frank Sinatra, meanwhile, in and out of retirement, tried to revive his gambling licence. In February 1981, he was questioned in front of the Nevada Gaming Control Board. President Reagan, along with Sinatra's Hollywood friends Gregory Peck, Kirk Douglas and Bob Hope, testified on his behalf that he wasn't in business with organized crime. And when Sinatra admitted having known Sam Giancana socially, but denied any business with the Mafia, the board approved his licence as an entertainment consultant for Las Vegas's Caesars Palace casino and hotel.

Above: Laynie Jacobs in court in 1991 when she was sentenced for murder. Eight years earlier she'd been a Mob-backed cocaine dealer in a relationship with a major Hollywood figure and had been hoping to become a producer.

> They drove into the desert
> where, in a remote canyon,
> Radin was shot 12 times. His
> body wasn't found for six weeks.

Cocaine and The Cotton Club Murder

Roy Radin's Hollywood connection began with a limousine ride. His life ended, a few months later, with another limousine ride when, on 13 May 1983, Laynie Jacobs, a business associate, who, like Radin, was trying to get into movies, invited him to dinner. She picked him up in a limousine from his Hollywood hotel, but instead of heading to a Beverly Hills restaurant, they set off in the other direction. Soon two bodyguards climbed into the limo and Jacobs skipped out. They drove north into the desert and sagebrush where, in a remote canyon, Radin was shot 12 times. His body wasn't found for six weeks.

Right: Conceived as '*The Godfather* with music', *The Cotton Club's* off-screen drama proved more interesting – one murder, three Las Vegas casino owners financing the film and an out-of-control budget.

Above: Chicago, 1934. Bank robber John Dillinger admitted that he was 'nuts about Clark Gable'. Followed on leaving the cinema on the left where he'd been to see Gable in *Manhattan Melodrama*, Dillinger was shot by federal agents in the alleyway on the right.

Radin had recently become connected to major Hollywood players when producer Robert Evans, the head of production at Paramount at the time of *The Godfather*, wanted to make a film noir with music and dancing centred around The Cotton Club nightclub. It would be a big-budget story about bootleggers. Now working as an independent producer, however, Evans had failed to find finance from the studios and was looking elsewhere for investment. Then one evening an unemployed dancer working as a limousine driver, Gary Keys, got talking to him. If Keys could help find some financing for the film, he'd be given a role, Evans promised.

Soon the dancer introduced Evans to Laynie Jacobs, who quickly became Evans's girlfriend and fellow cocaine snorter. She was, in fact, a thirty-something mid-level drug dealer from Miami, and she introduced Evans to 33-year-old Radin, who had made a lot of money in vaudeville shows of chimps, jugglers and down-on-their-luck celebrities. Radin was willing to invest and had connections to other potential investors. And, like Jacobs and Evans, he also had a cocaine habit.

MUTUAL ADMIRATION

THE MOVIES AND the Mafia have always fed off each other, with bank robber John Dillinger admitting learning how to wear his hat, how to swagger and how to hold a gun from repeated viewings of *Jesse James under the Black Flag* (1921). He was, he said, 'nuts about Clark Gable'. In fact, so 'nuts' about the star that he was followed to a cinema where he watched *Manhattan Melodrama* (1934), in which Clark Gable played a gangster on death row. On leaving the cinema, Dillinger was challenged by federal agents, attempted to flee and was gunned down.

Bugsy Siegel liked to socialize with famous actors and even had some personal screen tests made – though nothing came of it. After George Raft's success in *Scarface* (1932), a film based on the career of Al Capone and that glamorized mobsters, Siegel (pictured, below left, with Raft) even began to wear suits like Raft's character in the movie.

In *Scarface*, Raft, who'd grown up among gangsters in New York, was given a bit of business flipping a coin in one scene, whereupon several gangsters took it up to the point where it became a gangland trademark. Obsessed by the movie, Capone summoned Raft, wanting to know how closely the film was supposed to represent his life. After all, at the end of the film Scarface dies in a shoot-out with police. Raft reassured him the film was just fiction. As indeed it was. Capone developed dementia caused by syphilis and died following a heart attack in 1947.

As Warren Beatty, who played Bugsy Siegel on screen, said: 'Gangsters tried to copy Hollywood as much as Hollywood tried to copy gangsters … They were all part of the romantic swirl of American drama.' Even the term 'The Godfather' wasn't used among mobsters until Mario Puzo created it.

Hollywood is as popular as ever with the Mafia. Advances in film technology have made piracy easier, with DVD piracy offering a higher profit margin than any drug.

All was going well until Radin decided to cut Jacobs out of the film. Somehow he hadn't taken on board her Mafia connections who were supplying the cocaine. Jacobs thought that Radin had stolen a quarter of a million dollars and ten kilos of cocaine from her apartment, and now Radin had pushed her off the movie: she wasn't going to be a film producer after all. Radin was first offered $3 million to walk away from the movie, leave Hollywood and keep his life. But he wouldn't be persuaded. So, Jacobs organized Radin's limousine ride into the desert.

Years later, Laynie Jacobs was apprehended and in 1991 the case came to court. Robert Evans didn't testify as a witness, protected from possibly incriminating himself by pleading the Fifth Amendment. Jacobs and the hit men were sentenced to life for murder.

The Cotton Club did find financing in 1983 from Ed and Fred Doumani and Victor Sayyah, who were Las Vegas casino owners. The film went wildly over budget, was a flop at the box office and is now regarded as one of Hollywood's bigger disasters.

The Mob and Hollywood Today
It might seem that the age of the Mob and Hollywood is over, but Hollywood is as popular as ever with the Mafia. Advances in film technology have made piracy easier with, for example, illegal Chinese immigrants imported to Spain to burn pirate DVDs (one unit could burn 150,000 DVDs a day). Regarded wrongly by many as a victimless crime, DVD piracy has a higher profit margin than any drug. A DVD that can be made for 50 cents in the US can be sold in London for £5 ($8). It's also less risky than drug-

dealing. The piracy business is estimated by US government agencies to be worth up to $350 billion a year and some major films are now released globally on the same day to try and beat the pirates.

Nor is it only the Mafia who profit from piracy.

Right: Movies love mobsters, but mobsters also love movies. Warren Beatty (right) as mobster 'Bugsy' Siegel in *Bugsy* (1991), who extorted Hollywood studios but had private screen tests made, too.

Intellectual property crime has also become the preferred method of funding for some terrorist organizations, with illegal DVDs a major component. While buying a pirate DVD might seem as if it's only cheating a movie studio out of a little money, the question to ask is, where is the money going instead? Towards terrorism? To the Mafia? Ever since the Mafia muscled in on the unions in the 1930s, organized crime has found a way to make money out of Hollywood. It continues to do so.

In Hollywood sex can help a starlet to success, or occasionally become the trade
she plies if she doesn't make it; it can be the secret the star has to hide or
the indulgence the star can finally enjoy. Its appeal can make careers,
but it can also ruin them; it can be cut out of films, but not out of life.
And in Hollywood, where lives are heightened, the sex is always more extreme.

❖

'They can't censor the gleam in my eye.'

One might think that Hollywood films began tame and have become progressively more risqué, but in fact nudity was a popular feature of American cinema from its very early days. Theda Bara became known in the 1910s for vamp roles in exotic parts such as *The Queen of Sheba* and *Cleopatra*, in which she appeared in diaphanous robes and a bra seemingly made of serpents. While in a waterfall sequence in 1916's *A Daughter of the Gods*, Annette Kellerman appeared totally naked, with only her long

During the 1950s and 1960s Jayne Mansfield tried to follow in the wake of Marilyn Monroe as a peroxide blonde sex symbol, but never achieved the same degree of success. She was killed in a car crash in 1967.

hair to protect her modesty. And then, just as now, there were criticisms that the nudity was gratuitous.

But it wasn't just the women. Writer Elinor Glyn insisted that the men in her films in the 1920s would be seen in tight silk tights and without jockstraps. 'I do not believe in interfering with nature,' she explained. Necessary for the plot or not, Cecil B. DeMille was so taken with the first nude bathing scene he filmed in 1919's *Male & Female* that he ensured there was one in each of his next films.

Hays's Formula

So, if audiences, with a few vocal exceptions, were enjoying a bit of nudity or near-nudity in the melodramas, who stopped all the fun? Well, in part, Hollywood itself. After the scandals of Roscoe Arbuckle, Charlie Chaplin and William Desmond Taylor, the Dream Factory had not only become the spinner of stories, but the story itself. So when

Above: One way around the censors of the 1920s was to film classical stories about sinful characters who might ultimately be redeemed or punished. Pictured is Claudette Colbert bathing in ass's milk in *The Sign of the Cross* (1932).

President Harding's postmaster-general Will Hays was made president of the newly created Motion Pictures Producers and Distributors of America in 1922, his function was not only to clean up what Hollywood got up to off screen but on screen as well. The defence of artistic free speech in film had been lost in 1915, when the Supreme Court had declared that movies were not protected under the First Amendment, after which individual states began running their own censorship boards. Under Hays, the idea was that the film-makers would release their films already censored, and so they wouldn't need to be cut depending on different states' standards.

Hays quickly introduced a list of recommendations on suitable screen content, while a Doom Book was compiled of 117 Hollywood names deemed unsafe

At first the Hays list wasn't taken seriously: in *Queen Kelly* Gloria Swanson was seen taking off her knickers and throwing them at an army officer, who then caressed his face with them.

because of their no-longer-private lives. At first, Hays's list wasn't taken seriously by the industry – as seen in 1929's *Queen Kelly*, when Gloria Swanson was still taking off her knickers and throwing them at an army officer, who then caressed his face with them.

But when, the same year, a Jesuit priest, Fr Daniel A. Lord and a lay Catholic, Martin Quigley, editor of the *Motion Picture Herald*, proposed a new code as a means of the industry policing itself, changes did begin to take place. Not only did the code state what could be seen on screen, it also adopted a moral tone on the messages conveyed in films: thus adultery couldn't be portrayed as attractive, crime mustn't pay and authority should be respected. Cecil B. DeMille's reaction to this was to replace his more racy contemporary films about flappers with seemingly

---

Historian Thomas Doherty described Hollywood under the Production Code as 'a Jewish-owned business selling Roman Catholic theology to Protestant America'.

---

worthy Old Testament and ancient Roman subjects about sin, which still delivered a great deal of bare flesh, including a topless Claudette Colbert bathing in ass's milk in 1932's *The Sign of the Cross*.

The flouting of censorship finally ended, however, with the establishment of the Production Code Administration (PCA) in 1934, and for the next 30 years all American films required a certificate from the PCA to be released. Under Joseph Breen, who headed

the PCA for 20 years, on-screen married couples' bedrooms were to have two single beds, navels had to be covered and kisses couldn't last more than eight seconds – script girls had stopwatches to time them. And there were to be no inter-racial relations.

Even cartoons, such as *Betty Boop*, weren't exempt from the Production Code. The sexy jazz character in a cocktail dress was from the more liberal 1920s, but in the 1930s she became more demure with a less revealing dress, less jewellery and even fewer curls. Having lost the sharper edge to her character, her popularity shifted from adults to children.

So what changes did the Hays Office make to movies? One example: in the 1952 Broadway play *The Seven Year Itch*, a married man pursues and ultimately sleeps with a neighbour while his wife and son are away on holiday. In the film version, the Hays Office wouldn't allow his pursuit of his neighbour, played by Marilyn Monroe, to stretch beyond his longing and fantasy. George Axelrod and Billy Wilder, the playwright and the director of the movie, felt that these restrictions had left their film toothless.

Later, historian Thomas Doherty described Hollywood under the Production Code as 'a Jewish-owned business selling Roman Catholic theology to Protestant America'.

Above: Marilyn Monroe and Tom Ewell as her married neighbour in *The Seven Year Itch* (1955). The film-makers wanted to show a hairpin being found in the man's bed to indicate that he'd been adulterous, but the censors wouldn't allow it.

In screwball comedies the studios began producing feisty female characters who were equal, or superior, to their men.

Censorship, however, could have its virtues. 'When the censor objects to something,' said director Robert Mamoulian, 'you invent a different way of doing it that is much more interesting, much more erotic.' So as the film-makers of the 1930s were unable to make films that lingered on women's semi-naked bodies, they had to come up with something else, and in screwball comedies began producing feisty female characters who were equal, or superior, to their men. Rather than shy, pretty girls, the attractiveness of the women in *Bringing up Baby* and *His Girl Friday* was down to their intelligence and wit.

Below: Cary Grant and Katharine Hepburn in the comedy *Bringing Up Baby* (1938). Stricter censoring during the 1930s led Hollywood to develop intelligent, wittier roles for women.

TUT, TUT, TUT

MOVIES UNDER THE Hays Office had much in common with St Augustine of Hippo's famous prayer: 'Grant me chastity and continence, but not yet.' Herman J. Mankiewicz explained the screenwriting of the era:

'In a movie … the hero, as well as the heroine, has to be a virgin. The villain can lay anybody he wants, have as much fun as he wants, cheating and stealing, getting rich and whipping the servants. But you have to shoot him at the end.' As long as the film-makers ultimately delivered the virtues that the Hays Office required, they could get away with a lot of vices first.

That's what happens in the Chicago gangster film *Scarface* (1932). The Hays Office banned the script, but the film was shot anyway, and, when it was released, the producers dodged the censor by adding a subtitle: 'The Shame of a Nation' and an exhortation: 'This is an indictment of gang rule in America, and the careless indifference of the Government. What are you going to do about it?' By those few words, they seemed to distance themselves from the content of their own film, when in fact they were gleefully serving up 90 minutes of exciting gang warfare and violence. St Augustine would have understood.

Today, a similar hypocrisy remains with film-makers insisting that because they show the consequences of violence, they are justifying its graphic depiction. The truth is, many film-makers and audiences enjoy screen violence, just as they do screen sex.

THE RAZOR'S EDGE

PRODUCER DARRYL F. ZANUCK didn't want to cast Anne Baxter (pictured with Tyrone Power) in the role of sexy Sophie in *The Razor's Edge* (1946), because to him all women were either frumpy librarians or loose broads, and Anne Baxter was the former. So, a producer friend of Baxter's, Gregory Ratoff, lied to Zanuck that he'd slept with Baxter ... and had had a wild time. Surprised by this, Zanuck called Baxter in for a screen test and cast her in the role. She won an Oscar.

Ingrid Bergman

The great no-nos of Hollywood life are all sex-related: homosexuality, sex with a minor, and, previously, illegitimate pregnancies. Not only was the revelation of these damaging enough in the public eye, the Hays Office involved itself, too.

When the rumour circulated in December 1949 that Ingrid Bergman, who was still married to her first husband Petter Aron Lindström, was pregnant by Italian film-maker Roberto Rossellini, she received a letter from Joseph Breen: 'It goes without saying that these reports are the cause of great consternation among large numbers of our people who have come to look upon you as the first lady of the screen, both

Left: Ingrid Bergman with director and lover Roberto Rossellini in 1949. When it was revealed that Bergman, who was married, had become pregnant by Rossellini, she was hounded out of Hollywood.

> When talk circulated that Ingrid Bergman was pregnant by Italian film-maker Roberto Rossellini, the Hays Office urged her to deny the rumours.

individually and artistically ... Such stories will not only not react favourably to your picture, but may very well *destroy your career as a motion picture artist*. They may result in the American public becoming so thoroughly enraged that your pictures will be ignored, and your box-office value ruined.' The letter ended with Breen urging Bergman to deny the rumours, which she ignored.

Ingrid Bergman said: 'People saw me in *Joan of Arc* and declared me a saint. I'm not. I'm just a woman, another human being.'

Above: Errol Flynn flanked by his lawyers Jerry Giesler (left) and Robert E. Ford (right) at a court hearing for his statutory rape trial in November 1942. Peggy Satterlee, the teenager Flynn was accused of seducing, can be seen in the background.

Comment was even made on Capitol Hill. Senator Edwin C. Johnson of Colorado argued that Bergman had perpetrated 'an assault upon the institution of marriage'. Hollywood executives threatened not only to ban *Stromboli* (1950), the film she'd made in Italy with Rossellini during which they'd fallen in love, but also her recent Hollywood movies, including *Joan of Arc* (1948). 'If out of the degradation associated with *Stromboli*,' the senator said, 'decency and common sense can be established in Hollywood, Ingrid Bergman will not have destroyed her career for naught.' Ed Sullivan even chose not to have her on his TV show.

As a result of the scandal, Bergman was barred from Hollywood. She moved to Italy to be with Rossellini, had three children with him and made four further films with him. Of Hollywood, she said: 'People saw me in *Joan of Arc* and declared me a saint. I'm not. I'm just a woman, another human being.' Bergman had had earlier affairs, but the public hadn't known about them. Only after she'd separated from Rossellini, seven years later, was she able to return to America and resume her Hollywood career.

In Like Flynn

In his prime, in the late 1930s and early 1940s, Errol Flynn was a romantic leading man known for his swashbuckling roles, such as Robin Hood. But his sex life nearly ruined his career when he was accused of statutory rape. The first case in 1942 involved two girls. Seventeen-year-old Betty Hansen had been at a party the 34-year-old star had attended and although he admitted having spoken to her, he denied they'd had sex.

> The district attorney added the case of Peggy Satterlee, who'd spent a weekend on Flynn's yacht the previous year. Flynn admitted that she'd been on the yacht and in his autobiography wrote that he'd never asked her age.

To this charge the district attorney added the case of Peggy Satterlee, who'd spent a weekend on Flynn's yacht the previous year. Flynn admitted that she'd been on the yacht and in his autobiography wrote that he'd never asked her age. He almost certainly did have sex with her, although in court he denied it. Later on, it was revealed that she was over 18 at the time, anyway.

The grand jury found Flynn not guilty of both charges and he thought he was off the hook, but later that day he received a strange telephone call. A man identifying himself only as 'Joe' told Flynn that he'd been lucky in court and demanded $10,000 to be dropped at a designated LA spot. Ignoring the man's threat, Flynn put the phone down. Two days later, the DA's office overruled the grand jury's decision and proceeded with the rape charges.

Right: Peggy Satterlee in court showing photographs of her weekend on Errol Flynn's yacht. 'I knew those women would acquit him,' Satterlee later said of the jury. 'They just sat and looked adoringly at him as if he was their son.'

Flynn began to suspect that there were politics behind his case.

Unlike his predecessor, Buron Fitts, the new district attorney, John Dockwiler, hadn't had the studios' backing and was determined to make a break with Hollywood connections and seal a conviction for the first big movie name to cross his path. Flynn happened to be that man.

AFTER HOURS

WRITER GEORGE AXELROD helped busty Jayne Mansfield with her screen test for *The Wayward Bus* (1957). The climax of the test was where she'd rub her breast up against the camera lens. Axelrod had the test shown on the Bel Air circuit, where, as Axelrod said, 'producers and high level people in Hollywood had their own projection rooms and no after-dinner conversation and therefore showed movies every night'. She got the part.

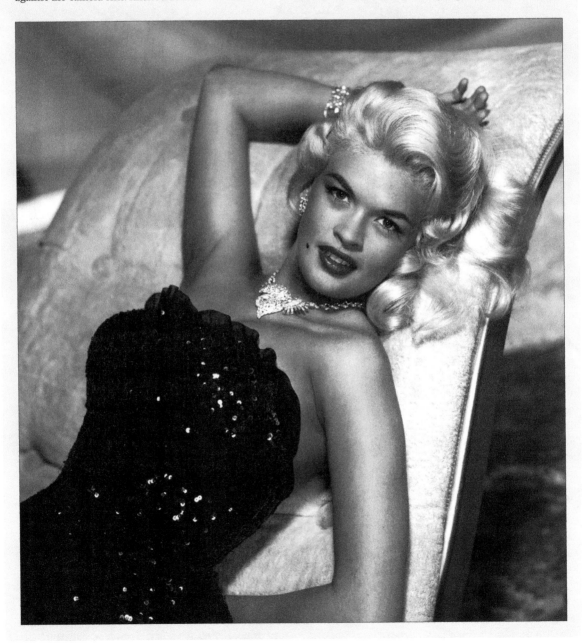

> Flynn had called Hansen's appearance 'gruesome' and reporters commented during the trial that she was, indeed, a rather plain-looking girl for a film star to take to bed.

At the court hearings, both girls dressed young, with Satterlee, who was in fact a dancer at a burlesque club in Los Angeles, arriving in bobby socks and pigtails. Flynn's lawyer, Jerry Giesler, pared away at the girls' stories, undermining their claims that they hadn't consented to sex. Flynn had called Hansen's appearance 'gruesome' and reporters commented during the trial that she was, indeed, a rather plain-looking girl for a film star to take to bed. Ultimately, the jury, largely made up of women, acquitted Flynn of all the charges.

Although Flynn found himself ostracized for a while in Hollywood, his career with Warner Bros. continued uninterrupted. Unlike Roscoe Arbuckle, whose career was ruined by a scandal in which he was found to be innocent, Flynn's scandal even provided a small boost at the box office, with audiences returning to his films to laugh at his movie *They Died with Their Boots On*. He'd been accused of having sex with Hansen with his shoes on.

Fraught though this time may have been, it didn't stop Flynn from noticing a slender girl at the courthouse's cigarette counter. Striking up conversation with her, he learnt that she was Nora Eddington and all of 18. What he didn't know at first was that her father worked in the LA County Sheriff's office. Nevertheless, she was of legal age and the following year, 1943, they married.

The Betty Hansen–Peggy Satterlee trial was only Flynn's first court case for statutory rape. On the night of Flynn's third wedding in 1950 in Nice, this time to 23-year-old Patrice Wymore, he was charged with having raped 17-year-old Denise Duvivier on his yacht in Monte Carlo the previous year. At the trial, Duvivier, whom Flynn said he'd never seen before, appeared, like Peggy Satterlee, looking as young as she could with her hair in pigtails. She'd claimed that they'd had sex in the shower, so Flynn, representing himself, showed the judge the tiny cubicle of a shower, which wouldn't have been able to fit two people, and the judge soon dismissed the case. While Flynn certainly liked girls of barely legal age, being a star also made him, and others, an easy target for false accusations.

It's also been suggested that Flynn liked boys, too, and that he and David Niven, friends known as great ladies' men, may have had a relationship. Marlene Dietrich, who enjoyed both men and women, heard from Carole Lombard that she'd found Flynn and Niven in bed together. 'None of us thought it such a big deal, though,' said Dietrich. 'Lots of actors slept with each other if there were no women around.'

Flynn was proud of his roistering and womanizing, writing in his autobiography in the final year of his life: 'My problem was not to get girls into my life, but to get them out.' But he always liked teenage girls. His companion when he died, aged 50, was Beverly Aadland. She was 17.

Cary Grant

Although Errol Flynn survived the statutory rape allegations, talk of another 'no-no' haunted Cary Grant's career – homosexuality.

Two days into Grant's first honeymoon in 1934, his marriage still hadn't been consummated. Instead, Grant took his bride, actress Virginia Cherrill, around

> Marlene Dietrich, who enjoyed both men and women, heard from Carole Lombard that she'd found Flynn and Niven in bed together.

New York, showing her his old haunts from his earlier theatre days in the city. When she made a joke about all the adolescent boys from England he'd had to live with, he told her stories about teenage boys comparing the sizes of their penises and rubbing themselves up against each other at night. To her, it was the closest he ever came to admitting that he was bisexual.

On reaching his New York home that weekend, Grant carried Virginia across the threshold, but their matrimonial moment was spoilt by her discovery that Randolph Scott, Grant's good friend, and, it was rumoured, former boyfriend, was not only still living there, but had no intention of moving out. Their marriage lasted only a year before Cherrill divorced him. Before Grant had moved to Hollywood, there'd been no talk of girlfriends in New York. He'd worked a little bit as a gigolo for wealthy women and had been close to George (Jack) Orry-Kelly, an openly gay set designer and later Hollywood costume designer, with whom he shared lodgings along with actor Lester Sweyd. But Broadway wasn't as high profile as Hollywood and Grant hadn't been a star there. Los Angeles was different. His early co-stars Marlene Dietrich, Tallulah Bankhead and Carole Lombard gossiped that he was gay and his studio, Paramount, had to counter this with magazine articles about him being a ladies' man.

When Louella Parsons in her newspaper column suggested that Grant was gay, he sued her for libel and they settled out of court, but the talk didn't go away. In the 1950s, his 25-year-old chauffeur, Raymond Austin, made a claim that he was the other man, Grant's lover, in one of Grant's divorces. A month later Austin tried to commit suicide and the claim disappeared. Then, in 1980, Grant sued Chevy Chase when he said of him on television: 'I understand he's a homo.' Again, they settled out of court. On the other hand, and when still married to Betsy Drake (wife number three), Grant and Sophia Loren fell in love while on location. He tried to woo her away from her husband, producer Carlo Ponti, but in the end she stayed.

Gay, straight or bisexual, Grant was a troubled man, which, given his childhood, might not be surprising. Born in Bristol, England, he was an only child, but his mother had suffered from depression since the death of a previous sibling. When Grant was nine, his father put his mother in a mental asylum and

Right: Cary Grant with his first wife Virginia Cherrill. Two days into their honeymoon their marriage hadn't been consummated, and when Grant carried her over the threshold of their new home, she was surprised to find that his friend Randolph Scott was still living there.

> Gay, straight or bisexual, Grant was a troubled man, which, given his childhood, might not be surprising.

told Grant that she'd gone away. Grant came to assume that she'd died. The following year, Grant's father abandoned him and left to marry another woman. It was only when Grant was 31 that he learnt his mother was alive and being looked after in a care home.

Grant married five times and had a daughter with his fourth wife. But even he said: 'All my wives except Betsy have accused me of being a homosexual.' There may have been rumours about his sexuality throughout his life, but Grant managed – and without the protection of a Hollywood studio because he worked independently from the late 1930s – to maintain a highly successful career.

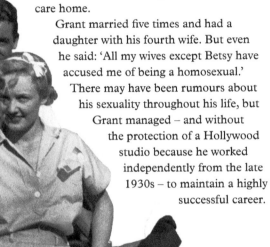

SEX ADDICTION

Surely Hollywood players, through attractiveness or money, can find as much sex as they desire? Well, not if they're addicted to sex, which might explain why actress Gloria Grahame ended up in bed with her teenage stepson.

Grahame (pictured below in 1955's *The Cobweb*) married director Nicholas Ray in 1948, but it seemed she required the constant validation from sex that she was still young (she was 27) and beautiful. When Ray's attention was insufficient, she'd go out and stay out. Suspecting that she was sleeping with other men, Ray hired private detectives to follow her.

Then, in the summer of 1951, Tony Ray, Nicholas Ray's 13-year-old son from his first marriage, came to stay at their Malibu home. According to biographer Vincent Curcio, Gloria Grahame and Tony made love that first afternoon and continued to do so for several days, before Ray barged in one afternoon to catch them together.

'I was infatuated with her,' Ray admitted years later, 'but I didn't *like* her very much.' Ray and Grahame divorced the following year, but for Gloria Grahame things may have ended happier than expected. In 1960, after a subsequent marriage, she married Tony Ray, nine years after their first affair. They remained together for 14 years and had two children. Of her four marriages, it was by far the longest.

Left: Diane Baker became one of a number of actresses who found themselves the subject of unwanted attention from Alfred Hitchcock. Apart from inviting her to lunch and trying to shock her with smutty conversation, the director also forced her to kiss him.

Hitchcock's Blondes

While directors such as *Casablanca*'s Michael Curtiz was said to have enjoyed sexual favours from extras behind the set, Alfred Hitchcock's relationships with some of his leading ladies were dreamier, but more sinister and unsatisfactory for both sides. Not only did he fall in love with Grace Kelly and Ingrid Bergman, a weakness many a man might well understand, he even insisted to others that Bergman had refused to leave his bedroom until he'd made love to her. No one believed him.

Over the years, however, Hitchcock began to try to realize these fantasy affairs. During the filming of *Marnie* (1964), he developed an affection for Diane Baker, one day appearing in her dressing room, kissing her straight on the lips, before being turned away – all, like a movie, without a word spoken. He'd also invite her for intimate lunches where he'd talk about sex and going to the toilet – having a smutty, and at times, cruel sense of humour. Later, while making his final film, *Family Plot* (1976), he surprised actress Karen Black, thrusting his tongue into her mouth.

But his most damaging obsession was with Tippi Hedren. Having seen the model in a TV commercial, Hitchcock decided that he'd make her his leading

Alfred Hitchcock fantasized about relationships with his actresses. He even insisted to others that Ingrid Bergman had refused to leave his bedroom until he'd made love to her. No one believed him.

'He reached over and violently embraced me to make everyone think that we were in a romantic clinch!'

lady for *The Birds* (1963). While claiming that he was nurturing a new talent, the director, now in his early sixties, had actually fallen in love with the 33-year-old. No other actor was allowed to share her car to the studio or mix with her on set. One day Hedren was in the car with him when, in her words, as they came into view of the crew, he 'reached over and violently embraced me to make everyone think that we were in a romantic clinch!' Hedren pushed him off and jumped out of the car.

Undeterred, Hitchcock would arrange for the two of them to have drinks together each day after work, meetings she tried to avoid. Smitten he might have been, but he was also cruel towards her. In a scene where her character is attacked by birds, Hitchcock told Hedren that they'd use mechanical birds. In fact, Hedren endured five days of live gulls, crows and ravens (with their beaks tied shut) being thrown at her. Traumatized, she was finally signed off work for a week by a doctor when her cheek was gouged by a bird and her eye was narrowly missed.

Their relationship reached breaking point on *Marnie*, their second, and final, movie together. On set one day, Hitchcock leaned across to Hedren. 'Touch me,' he whispered. 'His tone and glance made it clear what he meant,' she later said. 'I was disgusted.' On another day, Hitchcock called her into his office, explaining, 'as if it was the most normal thing in the world,' she said, 'that from this time on, he expected me to make myself sexually

Below: Hitchcock developed an obsession for Tippi Hedren. He controlled whom she spoke to on set, wouldn't allow others to travel with her to the studio, and, ultimately, told her that he expected her to make herself sexually available to him. She didn't.

available and accessible to him – however and whenever and wherever he wanted'.

Having endured Hitchcock for three years, Hedren had finally had enough, but when she told him that she wanted to break her contract, he suggested what to Hedren could 'only be described as prostitution'. After that, he began to threaten that he'd ruin her career. He did keep her under contract, paying her without using her or allowing her to work for anyone else. But the year after *Marnie* was released, he sold her contract on to Universal. He hadn't made her a star and he hadn't made her love him or have sex with him. Only on screen had he successfully resolved his sexual desires, frustrations and obsessions.

THE LONGEST KISS

ALTHOUGH UNDER THE Production Code, kisses were only allowed to be eight seconds long, in making *Notorious* (1946) Alfred Hitchcock designed the longest screen kiss of the time. By having his couple, Cary Grant and Ingrid Bergman, embrace and kiss for as long as allowed, pause, exchange a few words, nuzzle each other, kiss again, pause again and so on, the kiss lasted for two and a half minutes – 18 times longer than a single kiss was permitted.

The Casting Couch

We hear a lot about the casting couch, but did it really happen? Not only did it happen, but for Darryl F. Zanuck who was head of production at Warner Bros. in the early 1930s, it happened at 4 o'clock every day. Behind his studio office was a hidden boudoir with a tiger-skin bedspread. Every afternoon, at the allotted time, a starlet would be sent up for a half-hour meeting. It was seldom the same starlet twice.

So much for the couch, but what about the actual

Above: Head of production at Warner Bros. in the 1930s, Darryl F. Zanuck had a different starlet sent to his office every afternoon. Even if she accepted his sexual advances, there was no guarantee of work – for him there were plenty of starlets around.

casting? In fact, that was by no means a done deal. Having had his fun, Zanuck, or other producers and executives in positions of power, had no need to invest anything more in the starlet. If the executive became involved with the girl, however, or hoped to become

involved, that could lead to her being cast in a role. In later life, Zanuck left his wife and produced films featuring a series of younger lovers.

Harry Cohn at Columbia was also a notorious womanizer, while Louis B. Mayer would like to have been but lacked the personality for it. He made clumsy passes, developed crushes and was rather innocent when it came to sex, although he did manage a few affairs. 'I can make you the biggest star in the world in three pictures,' he promised Anita Page after she

> 'I can make you the biggest star in the world in three pictures,' he promised Anita Page after she rejected his advances. 'But, Mr Mayer, I'm already a star,' she said.

rejected his advances. 'But, Mr Mayer, I'm already a star,' she said. She was soon loaned out to other studios and by 1936 was out of the business. She wasn't willing to trade sex for stardom, while Mayer, it seems, wasn't willing to take rejection.

Nor is it always the person in a position of power making the advance. 'In my own 18 years as a studio executive,' wrote Peter Bart in *GQ* in 1996, 'I noticed that tactful "approaches" were made towards me not just by wannabe actresses but by women with scripts to sell, pictures to produce or projects to package.' Hollywood is populated by some aggressively ambitious men and women. Success can mean immense fame and wealth. For some of them, sex is just a means to that end.

Hollywood's Whores

Although movies might have become more moralistic after the introduction of the Hays Office rules, that didn't change the *behaviour* of Hollywood people. They just had to be more discreet. The hypocrisy of off-

Left: Having been a star who successfully made the transition from silent to talking pictures, Anita Page's career waned in the 1930s. She later claimed that refusing the sexual demands of MGM's Louis B. Mayer and Irving Thalberg had wrecked her career.

ITALIAN STALLION

BEFORE SYLVESTER STALLONE made his name with *Rocky* in 1976, he appeared in a softcore porn film, *The Party at Kitty and Stud's* (1970). Once he became a star, the porn film was quickly re-released under the title *Italian Stallion*. Although he appears nude in the film, by today's standards, says Stallone, the film would receive a PG rating. Broke and sleeping in a bus station when he was offered the work, Stallone said: 'It was either do that movie or rob someone because I was at the end – at the very end – of my rope.' For the two days' work it required, he was paid $200 and found himself somewhere to live.

screen vice but on-screen virtue actually increased.

Not all the pretty girls who headed to Hollywood made careers as actresses. Many, on arriving, realized that, while they'd been the prettiest girl in their small town, in Hollywood they were just one of hundreds and that there were others who were better actresses. Most just gave up, left town or did something else. But some became prostitutes and made a good living at it. On Sunset Strip in the 1930s, there was a brothel run by Lee Francis where Errol Flynn, Clark Gable, Spencer Tracy and Jean Harlow were among the customers. It's claimed that 40 per cent of the profits went to pay off police and politicians, but Francis's luck ran out in 1940 and she was convicted for running a house of ill repute. Around the same time, Mae's was a brothel where the girls were made up to look like movie stars, such as Marlene Dietrich, Jean Harlow and Ginger

> Many, on arriving, realized that, while they'd been the prettiest girl in their small town, in Hollywood they were just one of hundreds and that there were others who were better actresses.

Mae's was a brothel where the girls were made up to look like movie stars, such as Marlene Dietrich, Jean Harlow and Ginger Rogers.

Rogers. According to author E.J. Fleming, it was run for MGM by actress Billie Bennett, whose career had died with the coming of sound.

By the 1990s, the major brothels were run by Madam Alex Adams and Heidi Fleiss, who, though she wouldn't name other names, counted Charlie Sheen among her business's many Hollywood clients. 'In Hollywood, it's a status symbol to even have been on Alex's list of customers,' said writer William Stadiem, co-author of Adams's memoir *Madam 90210*. Men were happy to pay a few thousand dollars to meet a woman for the first time and then see if they could get her to sleep with him for free the second time.

Nor had the Fleiss women fallen into prostitution as a last resort. Among them, Stadiem met lawyers, accountants and development girls from the studios. 'They find it an amazing way to make a lot of money in a very short time,' he said. Fleiss's prostitutes have also succeeded in moving out of prostitution into Hollywood properly, becoming, it is said, producers, studio executives, actresses or models, as well as marrying men in the movie business.

Today, as much as ever, for some ambitious producers or studio executives too absorbed in work to embark on a proper relationship, hiring prostitutes has become accepted practice. In a community that values power and money so much, paying for sex can be just another business transaction.

End of the Production Code

After the studios lost control of many of the cinema circuits in the late 1940s, more independent exhibitors sprang up who would show foreign-language films, and, not being part of the Hollywood system, didn't have to comply with the Production Code. Then, in 1953, after the Supreme Court gave movies freedom of speech under the First Amendment, film-maker Otto Preminger defied the Production Code by distributing *The Moon is Blue* without its seal of approval. The Hays Office had wanted to change six lines of dialogue, but

Right: Hollywood madam Heidi Fleiss. When Charlie Sheen testified at Fleiss's tax evasion trial, he was asked if it was true he'd spent $50,000 on Fleiss's services. He grinned: 'It does add up, doesn't it?'

Preminger refused. The film went on to be a success.

As the Production Code was being successfully flouted and more risqué European films were being distributed in the US (such as the nudity seen in Ingmar Bergman's *Summer with Monika*, released in America in 1955), the studios themselves began to make more daring movies, adapting Tennessee Williams's plays *Cat on a Hot Tin Roof* (1958) and *Suddenly Last Summer* (1959), both of which dealt with homosexuality. As *Suddenly Last Summer* ends with a homosexual man being eaten by men he's trying to procure for sex, the Production Code felt that the film was sufficiently damning of homosexuality to allow it to be made into a movie.

While Billy Wilder hadn't been allowed in 1955 to suggest adultery in *The Seven Year Itch*, the whole subject of his film *The Apartment*, made just five years later, *was* adultery. The movie tells the story of an office worker who gains career advancement by loaning out his apartment to senior colleagues as a place to conduct their extra-marital affairs. It was an idea Wilder had had in the mid-1940s, but he'd known then that it wouldn't have been permitted by the Production Code.

As attitudes became more liberal throughout the 1950s and 1960s, the Production Code was undermined until it was replaced in 1968 with the ratings system based on ages, which, with amendments, remains today.

Roman Polanski

When director Roman Polanski was invited to guest edit an issue of the French edition of *Vogue* magazine in 1977, he approached 13-year-old Samantha

As the Production Code was being successfully flouted and more risqué European films were being distributed in the US, the studios themselves began to make more daring movies.

Above: William Holden, Maggie McNamara and David Niven in *The Moon Is Blue*, which, due to its 'unacceptably light attitude towards seduction, illicit sex, chastity and virginity' was released without the Production Code's seal of approval.

Invited to guest edit an issue of the French edition of *Vogue* magazine in 1977, Polanski approached 13-year-old Samantha Geimer...

Geimer (then Gailey) to do some modelling. With the permission of the girl's mother, the 43-year-old director took some photographs, and although Samantha later said she'd felt uncomfortable when he'd persuaded her to pose topless, she agreed to a second photo shoot.

During the second session, Polanski gave her champagne, which she was photographed sipping, and they shared a Quaalude sedative. As Polanski made sexual advances, she said that she protested, but had been scared. 'I didn't know what else would happen if I made a scene,' she said in an interview in 2003. 'After giving some resistance, I figured well, I

Right: Roman Polanski in 1977 after being sentenced to 90 days in a correctional facility. He was to be psychologically evaluated to determine whether his sentence for unlawful sexual intercourse with a 13-year-old should be more severe.

THE MANSON MURDERS

'I'M THE DEVIL, and I'm here to do the devil's business,' said Tex Watson as he broke into Roman Polanski's house in Benedict Canyon, Los Angeles, on 8 August 1969. Polanski was away, but his wife, model and actress Sharon Tate, was at home with three friends. Watson and his two associates, Susan Atkins and Patricia Krenwinkel, together with Linda Kasabian, who was the getaway driver, had been instructed by cult leader Charles Manson to destroy everyone in the secluded property.

Tate, who was eight and a half months pregnant, was stabbed 16 times; her friend Abigail Folger was stabbed 28 times; Folger's boyfriend Voytek Frykowski was shot and then stabbed 51 times, and celebrity hairdresser Jay Sebring was shot and stabbed seven times, while a passer-by, Steven Parent, was shot and killed.

It was a crime that shocked and frightened not only Hollywood, but the entire United States and beyond, and has since become seen as the moment the drug-taking, free-living era of the Sixties came to an end in an orgy of pointless violence.

In 1968 Charles Manson, 5ft 2in tall and having spent more than half his life in and out of young offenders' institutions and prisons, had recently managed to tap into the hippie scene. His ambition was to become a singer-songwriter, and one of his songs even appeared as a Beach Boys B-side after he temporarily befriended one of the group. But his real talent turned out to be the manipulation of unstable young minds, and soon he was collecting druggie drop-outs in San Francisco and LA.

Prophesying a black–white race war based on his insane interpretation of the Book of Revelation and

Below: Charles Manson on trial in 1970. The following month he carved an X into his forehead. The female defendants soon copied him.

Above: Sharon Tate's body is removed from her Los Angeles home following the Manson Murders in August 1969.

a unique reading of the Beatles' 1968 song 'Helter Skelter', Manson had a dark charisma so mesmerizing that at its largest, his 'Family', as the cult that had developed around him had become known, had 35 members.

The house where Polanski and Sharon Tate were living at the time of the murders was known to Manson as it had formerly been occupied by Terry Melcher, a record producer friend of the Beach Boys and the son of Hollywood singing legend Doris Day. But there seems little reason as to why Tate and her friends were targeted, or why the following day Manson and ten of his family murdered a supermarket executive, Leno LaBianca, and his wife Rosemary, a dress shop co-owner. The LaBiancas were completely unknown to Manson.

Even after being arrested, Manson's hold over the Family continued. Its members often acted in unison in the courtroom, while other members of the cult who hadn't been involved in the killings didn't quickly disband once Manson was no longer there to lead them. Manson and the others accused were eventually all given death sentences, commuted to life in 1972 when California banned the death penalty.

Five years after the murders, Polanski returned to Hollywood to film Robert Towne's screenplay *Chinatown*. In it, John Huston's villain says to Jack Nicholson's private detective: 'Most people never have to face the fact that at the right time and right place, they're capable of anything.' All it had taken for some Sixties' drop-outs to become mass murderers was to fall under the spell of Charles Manson.

> Polanski, a French citizen,
> fled to France. He hasn't returned
> to the US or Britain since, and
> France has denied requests to
> extradite him.

guess I'll get to come home after this.' Polanski, in his autobiography, argued that she wasn't unwilling and the probation report stated that there was evidence that she was willing. Nevertheless, she was 13, and Polanski performed oral sex on her, as well as having vaginal and anal sex.

Polanski was later arrested on multiple charges, including rape by use of drugs, perversion, sodomy, lewd and lascivious act upon a child under 14, and furnishing a controlled substance to a minor. In a plea bargain he pleaded guilty to unlawful sex with a minor, with the other charges being dropped. He was sentenced to serve 90 days at Chino State Prison, during which he was assessed by a psychiatrist to determine if he was likely to be a repeat offender.

The psychiatrist, the probation officer and the victim were all against Polanski having to serve a jail sentence and it was believed that he would receive probation. But as the court hearing drew closer, word spread that the judge had decided to sentence Polanski to imprisonment followed by deportation. Fearing this, Polanski, a French citizen, fled to France. He hasn't returned to the US or Britain since, and France has denied requests to extradite him.

Samantha Geimer sued Polanski in 1988 for sexual assault and they settled out of court, with part of the deal being that he hand over the photographs from the two sessions. Polanski has said publicly that he has regretted the incident, while Geimer has forgiven him: 'He made a terrible mistake, but he's paid for it.' Polanski has tried repeatedly to have the charges dropped, and, in 2009, Geimer filed to have the charges against him dismissed, saying that decades

Left: Nastassja Kinski as Tess of the d'Urbervilles in 1979. Seventeen at the time, Kinski was in a relationship with her director, Roman Polanski, who'd fled the US two years earlier while on bail for rape charges with a 13-year-old girl.

of publicity as well as the prosecutor's focus on lurid details continued to traumatize her and her family. In response, the judge admitted that there had been misconduct by the original judge, but Polanski would have to appear in court to apply for dismissal.

In September that year, more than 32 years after the assault, Polanski was arrested on arriving in Switzerland. While US authorities attempted to extradite him, he was placed under house arrest and only released the following July when the Swiss authorities rejected the extradition bill. In 2013, Geimer published her autobiography, subtitled 'A Life in the Shadow of Roman Polanski'. On the jacket, she used one of the photographs the director took of her.

> Samantha Geimer sued Polanski
> in 1988 for sexual assault and
> they settled out of court in 1993,
> part of the deal being that he
> hand over the photographs
> from the two sessions.

Despite this experience, youth remained Polanski's taste. After fleeing America, his next film was an adaptation of Thomas Hardy's novel *Tess of the d'Urbervilles*, starring 17-year-old Nastassja Kinski, with whom Polanski was having a relationship. His 1988 film *Frantic* co-starred Emmanuelle Seigner, who was 21 when she began a relationship with the then 54-year-old film-maker. They married and have two children.

Woody Allen

Throughout the 1980s, Woody Allen's girlfriend was actress Mia Farrow, who appeared in all his films at the time. They didn't live together, but had a son together, born Satchel Farrow in 1987, and adopted two children, Dylan and Moshe (now Moses). Farrow had also already adopted three other children, including a daughter, Soon-Yi.

In 1992, Farrow found photographs Allen, then 56, had taken of the then 19-year-old Soon-Yi posing naked. It was then revealed that Allen had begun a sexual relationship with Soon-Yi. As Farrow and Allen

CELEBRITY SEX TAPES

BEFORE THE DEMOCRATIC National Convention in Atlanta, Georgia, in 1988, Rob Lowe met two girls at a bar, and, later that night, filmed them having sex with him. One of the girls was only 16. The girls stole the tape and when the younger girl's mother found it, charges were pressed.

Lowe settled out of court. A new type of scandal had been born: the celebrity sex tape. Lowe later quipped that being the first to do something is not always an honour.

Later sex tapes scandals would involve Pamela Anderson and her first husband Tommy Lee (below), Colin Farrell and a Playboy model, and Jennifer Lopez and her first husband Ojani Noa. For film stars the advice might be: 'Don't film yourselves having sex, because the tape might find its way into the wrong hands'. But for others lower down the greasy pole of fame one might question how unintentional it is that footage of their private life has suddenly put them in the news again.

broke up, a vicious custody battle began. It was alleged that Allen sexually molested Dylan, then aged eight, when he had visited the family at Farrow's home in Connecticut in August 1992. Farrow was out at the time, but there were other family members and babysitters around. Allen has always strongly denied the allegation and the New York Department of Social Services found no credible evidence to support the allegation, concluding that Dylan most likely made up the incident as a result of the disturbed family life or was coached by Farrow, or a mix of both. That said, Allen had been in therapy for alleged inappropriate behaviour around Dylan. Ultimately, the state attorney said that he had 'probable cause' to press charges against Allen, but declined as he didn't want to put the traumatized child on the stand. This left both Allen and Farrow losers: he wasn't tried, but was still smeared by the state attorney's 'probable cause' words.

Subsequently, the film-maker's application to win sole custody of Dylan, Moses and Ronan failed. The judge ruled that Allen's behaviour towards Dylan was 'grossly inappropriate' and that he

Above: Woody Allen and his wife Soon-Yi Previn in 2011. She is the adopted daughter of his ex-girlfriend Mia Farrow, as well as being step-sister to Farrow and Allen's son Ronan, and two children that they jointly adopted.

would have no visitation rights at all with his adopted daughter. 'This was a brutal blow to me, a cruel deprivation for Dylan, but the successful culmination of You took my daughter, now I'll take yours,' Allen wrote in 2020.

Throughout the 1990s, though, it was the relationship with Soon-Yi – they married and adopted two children – that drew more interest than the child

> Ultimately, the state attorney said that he had 'probable cause' to press charges against Allen, but declined as he didn't want to put the traumatized child on the stand.

molestation allegation. And while the implosion of Allen's relationship with Farrow may have tainted his reputation, movie stars from Julia Roberts to Cate Blanchett to Joaquin Phoenix were still keen to work with him. He remained as productive as ever – a movie every year – and with 2011's *Midnight in Paris* he achieved his biggest box office hit ever.

But, as adults, Dylan and Ronan repeated the molestation allegation, and, along with Ronan now working as a journalist, the accusation began to gain a traction that it hadn't 20 years earlier. And then, in 2017, came the fall of producer Harvey Weinstein and the explosion of the #MeToo movement...

King Harvey and his Court

'If Harvey Weinstein invites you to a private party in the Four Seasons, don't go,' was actress and musician Courtney Love's advice to young actresses in 2005. People outside Hollywood wouldn't have known what she was referring to, but rumours had long circulated about his mistreatment of women. Ten years later, journalists tried to investigate the rumours, but hadn't found women willing to go on the record, while a 2015 police investigation into a groping accusation against the producer hadn't led to a criminal charge.

Then, in 2017, Jodi Kantor and Megan Twohey of the *New York Times* tried and, gradually gaining the trust of actresses and former employees of Weinstein at his

> 'If Harvey Weinstein invites you to a private party in the Four Seasons, don't go,' was actress and musician Courtney Love's advice to young actresses in 2005.

THE FALL OF KEVIN SPACEY

THE TERM 'ME TOO' had been coined by sexual assault survivor and activist Tarana Burke in 2006, but following the allegations against Harvey Weinstein, it spread rapidly as a hashtag on social media. A few weeks after the Weinstein story broke, actor Anthony Rapp accused Kevin Spacey of making a sexual advance towards him in 1986, when Rapp was only 14. Spacey immediately apologized for his 'drunken behaviour', but, as with Weinstein, Rapp's speaking out prompted other men to bring allegations of sexual misconduct against the star. At the time, Spacey was the lead actor and executive producer of Netflix's political drama series *House of Cards*, as well as being a highly respected stage actor and double Oscar winner. Within days, it was announced that the next

series of *House of Cards* would be the last and Spacey was quickly written out. Meanwhile, he had already completed filming the supporting role of J. Paul Getty in the movie *All the Money in the World*, but, with the film-makers anxious that the scandal around the actor would hurt the movie, his scenes were reshot with Christopher Plummer less than a month before the film's release.

Five years later, Spacey hadn't made a Hollywood movie or TV series or starred in a play, though, with cases still being heard in the UK, he still hadn't been convicted of anything.

Below: In October 2022, Kevin Spacey was found not guilty of the sexual abuse of actor Anthony Rapp when Rapp was 14.

production companies Miramax and The Weinstein Company, published their story. They revealed that the producer had, over three decades, sexually harassed women and had paid settlements to eight former employees, binding them to non-disclosure agreements so that they could never speak publicly about the events. Days later, Ronan Farrow published a similar investigation into Weinstein in *The New Yorker*.

Weinstein's pattern of behaviour had been to invite an actress to a hotel restaurant to discuss a role, but, to her surprise, the meeting's venue at the last minute would often be changed to the producer's suite. There, he might greet her only wearing his dressing gown and soon ask for a massage or a shower. 'I said no, a lot of ways, a lot of times, and he always came back at me

> With Harvey Weinstein aware of the investigations into him during 2017, he employed the firm Black Cube to provide intelligence to stop negative stories appearing.

with some slimy ask,' remembered actress Ashley Judd of one encounter with Weinstein. Then, he'd play on his heft within the industry, saying that he could make or ruin an actress's career depending on whether she complied or not. Junior assistants called to his hotel room would be similarly treated. Zelda Perkins, one of those harassed assistants who had agreed a financial settlement with the producer, later said: 'He is pathologically addicted to conquering women.'

Gwyneth Paltrow remembered meeting Weinstein in his hotel suite early in her career. They talked business for a while, before the producer placed his hands on hers, asking her to exchange massages with him in his bedroom. He repeated the request, but she excused herself.

She immediately told her then boyfriend, Brad Pitt, who soon confronted Weinstein, warning the producer to keep his hands to himself. Weinstein later rang Paltrow, berating her for having told Pitt and threatening that he was going to ruin her career. He

didn't and Paltrow went on to star in *Emma* and won an Oscar for Miramax's *Shakespeare in Love*.

Over the years, Weinstein had worked hard promoting philanthropic endeavours, developing press contacts and cosying up to politicians, such as the Clintons – burnishing the reputation of a man presenting himself as bullish but ultimately on the right side. And during the 1990s and 2000s, he had distributed or helped finance such successful films as *The Crying Game*, *Pulp Fiction* and *The English Patient*, and had masterminded awards campaigns. After Steven Spielberg, he's the most thanked person in Oscar acceptance speeches of the past 50 years. At the same time, staff described him as 'abusive and bullying'. 'Working at Miramax in the late 1990s was like being in a cult,' remembered producer Paul Webster. 'The cult of Harvey.' Looking back, Webster reflected, many of the staff at Miramax, in turning a blind eye, had been Weinstein's enablers.

With Weinstein aware of the investigations into him during 2017, he employed the firm Black Cube to provide intelligence to stop negative stories appearing. Despite his efforts, when the story broke, more women went on the record, with more than 100, including Salma Hayek and Angelina Jolie, alleging that Weinstein had sexually assaulted them, and more than 20, including Rose McGowan, accusing him of rape. Within weeks, his second wife, Georgina Chapman, had left him and he'd been fired by the company he'd founded with his brother Bob. Six months later, The Weinstein Company filed for bankruptcy.

Weinstein always denied any allegations of non-consensual sex, but in February 2020, he was found guilty in New York of one count of rape and one count of sexual assault and sentenced to 23 years in prison. In June 2022, he was also charged in London with two counts of sexual assault against a woman in 1996, and in September 2022, an additional trial began in Los Angeles charging him with 11 counts of rape and also sexual battery.

The Weinstein Effect
Previously, women and men hadn't spoken out as much about sexual misconduct because either they felt that this was just the way of Hollywood, or that they wouldn't be believed, or would be charged with defamation. Following Weinstein's fall, a number of women made allegations – some on Twitter – against,

Above: Harvey Weinstein arriving at court in New York in February 2020. He would be found guilty of one count of rape and one count of sexual assault, and sentenced to 23 years in prison.

among others, *Toy Story* director John Lasseter, who was accused of 'grabbing, kissing and making comments about physical attributes' of staff at Pixar Animation. The leave of absence that Lasseter took from running Pixar in November 2017 became permanent the following year. When allegations of sexual assault and harassment were made against Brett Ratner, Warner Bros. ended its deal with the director, though no charges came to court. Actor Jeffrey Tambor resigned from the television show *Transparent* following allegations of sexual misconduct from a former assistant and from a co-star. Tambor apologized 'if any

action of mine was ever misinterpreted by anyone as being sexually aggressive' and he admitted having anger issues, but he denied being a predator.

In light of the #MeToo movement, attention turned again to Roman Polanski and Woody Allen. The known facts about the scandals in those film-makers' lives hadn't changed, but the public perception was shifting. Kate Winslet had in recent years worked

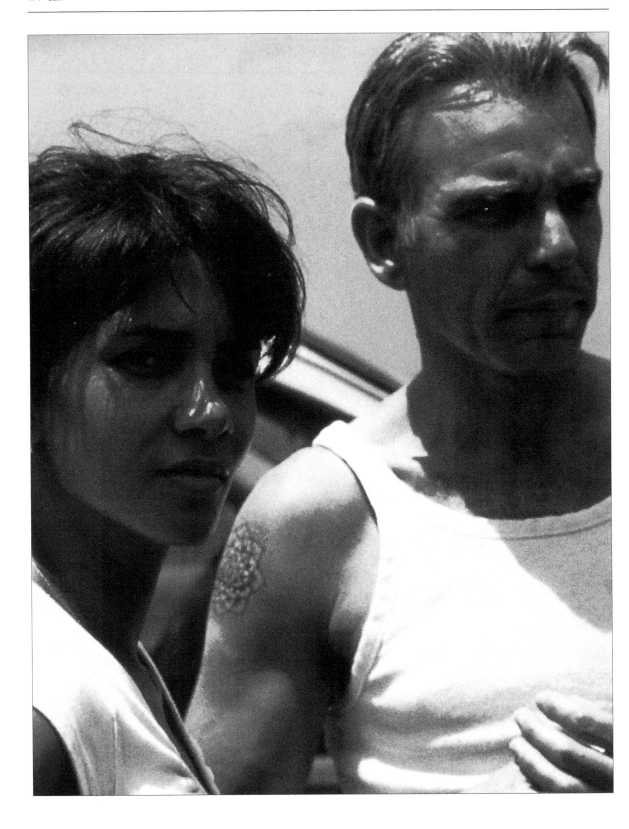

Left: Halle Berry and Billy Bob Thornton in 2001's *Monster's Ball*, which showed that more risqué inter-racial love stories featuring Hollywood names could be made, albeit as independent productions rather than by major studios.

with both and had described Allen as 'an incredible director'. Of the allegations, she had said: 'As the actor in the film, you just have to step away and say, I don't know anything, really, and whether any of it is true or false.' Three years later, these were her words: 'What the f**k was I doing working with Woody Allen and Roman Polanski?' Where Emma Stone and Colin Firth also now said that they regretted having worked with Allen, others, such as Scarlett Johansson and Penelope Cruz, came to his defence.

There were further negative consequences for Allen's career. Amazon Studios had financed but now refused to distribute his 2018 film *A Rainy Day in New York* and cut short its long-term deal with the film-maker. And when Allen's autobiography was scheduled to be published by an imprint of publisher Hachette, Ronan Farrow, whose own book about the conspiracy to protect sexual predators had been published by Hachette the previous year, protested. Following a staff walk-out, Hachette dropped Allen's title from its list. Arcade, a much smaller publisher, later issued Allen's book. Again, Allen had never been charged with anything, but in the eyes of many the film-maker had been found guilty.

A Brighter Future

Recent years have, though, seen some positive changes for women in Tinseltown. When Geena Davis – best known as Thelma in *Thelma & Louise* – began watching kids' movies with her children, she noticed how few roles there were for women. Sponsoring some research, she learned that female characters in children's movies and television were outnumbered by male characters three to one, that they were often hypersexualized and that the proportion who had roles in the workforce was lower than in reality. 'In other words,' she wrote, 'however abysmal the numbers in the real world were, they were far worse in *fiction* – where you *make it up*.'

In 2004, she launched the Geena Davis Institute on Gender in Media, which advocates for equal representation of women on screen. By pushing for change in children's entertainment, she hoped not to unconsciously train another generation to see girls

and women as secondary. In 2019, Davis received her second Oscar: this time, the Jean Hersholt Humanitarian Award for her efforts towards gender parity. By 2021, the institute's work had helped achieve gender parity for major and minor characters across Hollywood's children's films and television.

Following the #MeToo movement, another positive step was the introduction of intimacy co-ordinators on set to ensure the well-being of actors in sex scenes. Thirdly, the Time's Up Legal Defense Fund, which supports people who have been subject to workplace sex discrimination, was founded in the months after #MeToo rose to prominence.

When it was revealed that Mark Wahlberg had been paid $1.5 million for eight days' work on reshoots of *All the Money in the World*, while the film's lead, Michelle Williams, had received only $80 per diems, Wahlberg donated his fee to the fund. Even taking into account that Wahlberg was at the time mainly known for the phenomenally financially successful *Transformers* movies while Williams was respected for

---

Despite the end of the Production Code, today's Hollywood studios self-censor the inter-racial relationships in their movies.

---

roles in independent dramas, this was a gross example of the pay discrepancy between actors and actresses in Tinseltown. A huge pay discrepancy still exists between male and female actors in Hollywood; at least now there is greater awareness of it.

Sex Today

Hollywood cinema may be more liberal today than during the years of the Production Code, but it remains conservative in its attitude to on-screen sex or nudity. In contrast to much of Europe, Tinseltown's censors are stricter on sexual content than on screen violence. Off-screen, the scandals of recent years have, like the establishment of the Hays Office in the early 1920s, shaken up the Dream Factory. Time will tell how well the studios manage the industry's heady concoction of money, fame and beauty in the 21st century.

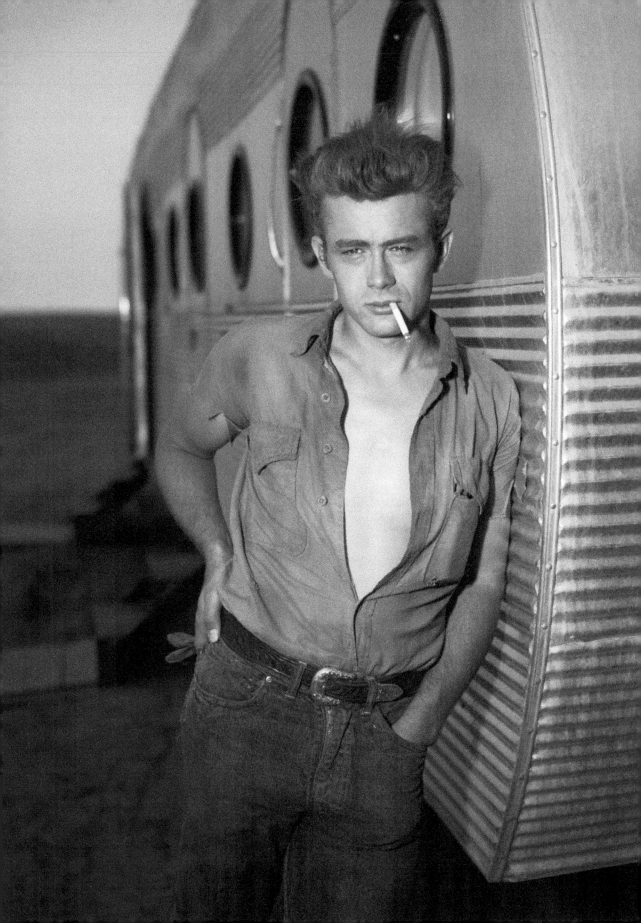

VII

STARS

Movie stars might be adored by millions, but some of them can struggle to love or be loved for themselves. By playing heroes on screen and treated like monarchs off screen, their view of the world can sometimes become warped. And success doesn't necessarily calm their fears; it can magnify them, too.

◆

'Stars don't have friends, they have people who work for them.'

What is it that creates the world's most desired sex symbol? Who knows? Marilyn Monroe's grandfather died when syphilis infected his brain. Her grandmother, Della, who may also have had syphilis, suffered from depression. Monroe's mother, Gladys, also suffered from depression after her violent, alcoholic husband took their two children and left. Her third child, Marilyn, or Norma Jeane as she was then known, didn't know who her father was. Gladys said Charles Stanley Gifford

One of Hollywood's most famous faces, James Dean became a star in 1955 with the release of his first film *East of Eden*. He died in a car crash months later, before his two subsequent films had been released.

Sr, with whom she worked at a film lab, was Monroe's father, but he denied it. Suffering from depression after Monroe's birth, Gladys was persuaded to allow a neighbour to foster the girl.

What followed was a childhood where Monroe was bounced between the neighbour, who had her until she was seven, and Glady's friend Grace McKee. Then came foster parents, orphanages, and, when she was well enough, Gladys herself. At 15, Monroe was a budding beauty, but with her foster parents leaving California and moving back East, it appeared that she was destined for the orphanage again. Instead, the mother of James Dougherty, a young man five years Monroe's senior, was approached. Dougherty had been on a few dates with Monroe and it was suggested that if Dougherty married Marilyn, she'd be saved from going back to the orphanage. So Dougherty married her not out of love or passion for the future sex symbol, but almost, it seems, as a favour; while Monroe married to

Above: In marrying when she was 16, Marilyn Monroe avoided being sent back to an orphanage. Then, while working in a munitions factory during World War II, she was discovered by a photographer and began her modelling career.

escape being a child. Marilyn Monroe, the 16-year-old housewife, was barely desired at all. And mentally she was already unwell. Like her mother, Monroe heard voices throughout her life and imagined sinister figures lurking outside her house.

Left alone while her husband was away during World War II, she began working in a munitions factory, where a photographer who was taking some publicity shots suggested she pursue modelling work. Quickly, her modelling career took off and she changed her hair from her natural brunette to a golden blonde.

Returning from the war, Dougherty didn't like his wife's new career path and told Monroe she had to decide between it and him. She chose her career.

> Like her mother, Monroe heard voices throughout her life and imagined sinister figures lurking outside her house.

Modelling brought her to the attention of Hollywood and she was signed on a short contract to Twentieth Century Fox.

Joseph Schenck, the studio executive who'd earlier been imprisoned for a pay-off scandal with the unions, was then the 69-year-old president of the studio. Throwing a party, he asked for some Fox girls to act as window-dressing and among the crowd Monroe caught his eye. Soon they began an affair, but her six-month contract with Fox wasn't renewed and nor was a subsequent one with Columbia.

Older, powerful Hollywood men would continue to feature in her life, and she began an affair with Johnny Hyde, a 53-year-old agent, who left his wife for her, and negotiated a seven-year contract with Fox. Still hearing voices, however, she took barbiturates to calm her anxieties, and when Hyde died of a heart attack, made her first suicide attempt, overdosing on pills.

As her career developed, her appeal emerged as a mix of sexuality and innocence, 'a kind of elegant vulgarity' as director Billy Wilder called it. She didn't have great range as an actress, but that is a part of star quality – stars don't disappear into new roles but mainly play variations on the same role. By the mid-1950s, both Hollywood and Monroe herself had discovered her star quality.

Her two later marriages were fraught. She married Joe DiMaggio at the beginning of 1954, but he wanted her to retire from acting to be his wife, and by the end of the year they'd separated. It's believed he was violent towards her, too. Following that, she had a relationship with Frank Sinatra, before marrying Arthur Miller. But soon both Monroe and

Right: Marilyn Monroe, with her lawyer Jerry Giesler, announces her divorce from baseball star Joe DiMaggio in October 1954, citing 'conflicting careers'. The marriage had lasted less than a year.

Miller, who, it's said, nagged her with criticisms, began having doubts about the person they'd married. After her divorce from Miller in 1961, she slipped further into depression, considered suicide and was persuaded to check herself into hospital.

When it came to her work, she famously had huge stage fright and was a testing collaborator. 'She was absolutely perfect,' said Billy Wilder, who directed her in *The Seven Year Itch* (1955) and *Some Like It Hot* (1959), 'when she remembered the lines'. While on some occasions she could complete a three-minute scene perfectly in the first take and immediately understood the humour behind it, at many other times remembering the lines could be a huge problem for

> After her divorce from Miller, Monroe slipped further into depression, considered suicide and was persuaded to check herself into hospital.

her. On *Some Like It Hot,* she required 50 takes just to say: 'Where's that bourbon?'

Not only was she difficult, she was often absent, sometimes not arriving until the afternoon. When she became pregnant during the shooting of *Some Like It Hot,* Arthur Miller told Wilder he shouldn't give Monroe a call-time before 11 in the morning. Exasperated, Wilder glared at him: 'She's *never* on set before 11 o'clock.'

Below: 'The most unlikely marriage since the Owl and the Pussycat,' commented a magazine of the 1956 wedding of Arthur Miller to Marilyn Monroe. He was a politically minded playwright; she'd been *Playboy's* first Playmate. Within weeks, both were having doubts.

KNICKERS

IN HER MOST famous movie scene in *The Seven Year Itch,* Marilyn Monroe walks along a New York street one summer night and cools herself by standing over a subway grating, holding her skirt down as the wind blows it up. Her then husband, Joe DiMaggio, was watching the filming and didn't approve – 'every time her dress blew up, he looked away,' said the movie's director Billy Wilder. DiMaggio left in a huff, but Monroe loved the attention she was receiving from the crowd that had gathered.

Almost 40 years later, Sharon Stone went further, agreeing to be filmed knickerless in a scene where she uncrosses and recrosses her legs in *Basic Instinct* (1992). As with Monroe, it turned out to be the most famous scene of the movie, but for Stone it became the only really famous moment of her career. After she saw the finished film, she claimed that she'd been misled and that she was shocked at how close-up the shots were.

From a movie where Monroe showed her knickers to a movie with a knicker-free Sharon Stone, what next? A knicker-free reality. In 2012, photographs of Anne Hathaway climbing out of a car at the New York première of the *Les Misérables* movie revealed that she wasn't wearing any underwear at all. Similarly, Eva Longoria, in hitching up her dress out of the puddles at the Cannes Film Festival in 2013, shared with the public that she was without knickers. Lifting their skirts is always going to win girls some attention, at least for a while.

Were Hathaway and Longoria not wearing any underwear because it would have ruined the lines of their dresses? Or had they both just been forgetful on those busy days and not put any on? The wardrobe malfunctions certainly made headline news, but not everyone believes that they were accidental.

Much has been made of her relationship with the Kennedys, especially by Monroe. It seems that Monroe spent the weekend with President John F. Kennedy in Palm Springs in March 1962 – the weekend he couldn't stay with Frank Sinatra because of Sinatra's Mob connections. While witnesses said it was obvious the two were intimate, that weekend was the extent of their relationship – two nights at most.

After their weekend, Monroe repeatedly rang the White House, but the calls weren't returned, with the President distancing himself from her. According to Kennedy's friend, Senator George Smathers, Jackie Kennedy was 'disgusted' that her husband had had a relationship with the troubled movie star and asked him to 'have some pity' on the girl. The following month, Monroe took an overdose of pills.

She later had dinner with Bobby Kennedy, among others, which, just as she'd created sob stories as a teenager to win sympathy, she talked up as 'a date with Bobby Kennedy'. Despite her claims, most insiders don't believe that Monroe and Bobby Kennedy had an affair.

In June that year she was fired from her final film, *Something's Got to Give*, having missed so many days' shooting due to illness that the film was now well behind schedule. 'The girl was neurotic beyond description,' said one of the film's screenwriters, Nunnally Johnson. 'She kept retreating further and further from reality.'

Two months later, in the early hours of 5 August 1962, Monroe was found dead from a barbiturates overdose. She was

Right: Marilyn Monroe on the set of her final, uncompleted film, *Something's Got to Give*, in 1962. Repeatedly absent from the production because of health problems, she was eventually fired. Two months later she died of a barbiturates overdose.

36. Despite the conspiracy theories that the FBI bumped her off because she had information on the Kennedys, the only suspicious element to her death was that after her doctor found her body, the authorities weren't called for two hours. She'd overdosed twice before in the previous month (once at Frank Sinatra's club at Cal Neva) and had been revived by friends. This was just the final step on a downward spiral.

Apart from *Some Like It Hot*, which, 50 years after her death, is considered a classic, none of her films is screened much or even rated that highly. Film historian David Thomson has suggested that Monroe was the first modern celebrity, as opposed to star, in that she's more famous for herself than for her film roles.

After she died, Whitey Snyder, her make-up designer, and his wife, Marjorie Lecher, a wardrobe mistress, fulfilled an old agreement with Monroe to make her up for the open casket. To their surprise, they found that her breasts had dropped. 'Marilyn without a bust,' said Snyder. 'She'd have freaked.' With padding and make-up, they recreated her famous look for her final appearance.

Marlon Brando

Although Marilyn Monroe hired Paula Strasberg from the New York Actors' Studio as her coach, she never became part of that world. Others stars from the Actors' Studio – Marlon Brando, James Dean, Montgomery Clift – changed screen-acting for good. Their movie careers, however, free from the paternalistic constraints of the studio system, were marred by their own recklessness and addictions.

Marlon Brando's early success in

> Making *Last Tango in Paris*, Brando hadn't learnt his lines and would rely on hidden cue cards as prompts.

Tennessee Williams's *A Streetcar Named Desire* on stage and screen and the movie *On the Waterfront* didn't sustain throughout his career. While no star can be expected to follow success with repeated success, Brando seemed to lose interest in acting. He was the first actor to be paid $1 million for a movie with 1960's *The Fugitive Kind*, but the 1960s also saw him star in a series of box-office failures and now largely forgotten films. By the time he was cast as Don Vito Corleone in *The Godfather* (1972), he might still have been regarded as the world's greatest screen actor but he had a reputation for being difficult and box-office poison. Initially Paramount didn't want him for *The Godfather*, but he was cast and won an Academy Award for his role. Controversially he then refused to appear at the ceremony, sending Sacheen Littlefeather, in Apache dress, to make a statement criticizing Hollywood's depiction of Native Americans.

In the same year, when he starred in the sexual drama *Last Tango in Paris*, it might have seemed that, although now in his fifties, his career was back on track. But again his attention didn't last. He hadn't learnt his lines and would rely on cue cards hidden out of view of the camera as prompts.

When it came to collaborating again with *The Godfather*'s director Francis Ford Coppola on *Apocalypse Now* (1979), Brando was asked to lose weight for the part of a renegade Special Forces officer, and to read Joseph Conrad's *Heart of Darkness*, on which the movie was loosely based, as preparation. Instead, Brando arrived on location overweight without

Below: Marlon Brando won an Oscar in 1973 for his role in *The Godfather*, but refused to appear at the ceremony. Instead he sent Sacheen Littlefeather (right) to read out a statement about Hollywood's misrepresentation of Native Americans.

REBEL WITHOUT A CAUSE

REBEL WITHOUT A CAUSE (1955) tells the story of three troubled teenagers in LA over one 24-hour period. By the time of the film's release, its star, James Dean, was already dead, while its two other principal actors, Natalie Wood and Sal Mineo, would also become closely identified with the movie and die young.

Dean's face is world-famous, his influence as an actor is huge, and yet he made only three films. After the smooth delivery actors gave in movies during the studio system, Dean, like Brando, spoke and moved the way people did in real life. Dean's most notable roles were playing two disaffected youths in the same year, in *East of Eden* and *Rebel Without a Cause*, but then his career ended before he had a chance to play much else. Speeding to a race event in his new sports car, he was killed in a crash aged 24.

After *Rebel Without A Cause*, Mineo (below left) struggled to escape playing teenage delinquent roles and his career foundered in the 1960s. Openly gay, his career had begun to pick up in his mid-thirties, but in 1976 he was stabbed to death outside his house by a pizza deliveryman.

Natalie Wood's other most notable roles were in *Splendor in the Grass* and as Maria in *West Side Story* (both 1961), before moving into television and taking time off to have children. But in 1981, the 43-year-old star was making movies again, and, with her co-star Christopher Walken and her husband Robert Wagner, sailed to Catalina Island on her yacht for an evening. By the following morning, Wood had drowned, her body being found a mile away, with a dinghy from the yacht nearby.

No one said they'd seen Wood enter the water, although Wagner later admitted that he'd had a fight with his wife that night. There was a scratch across her cheek and bruising on her torso and arms, which the coroner suggested as possibly being caused by slipping while trying to climb back aboard the boat. Along with having alcohol in her blood that was twice the drink driving limit, she had taken a motion sickness pill and a painkiller, which would have increased her sense of intoxication.

Her death was declared an 'accidental drowning', but in 2011 the yacht's captain, Dennis Davern, said that he'd lied on his first statement to the police and a new investigation was begun. In 2012, the death was reclassified as caused by 'drowning and undetermined causes'.

having read the book or, again, having learnt his lines. Rather than act, he would engage Coppola in long discussions about his character when they should have been shooting. 'I was good at bullshitting Francis,' wrote Brando, 'but what I'd really wanted from the beginning was to find a way to make my part smaller so that I wouldn't have to work so hard.' Not looking convincing as a menacing soldier, he was replaced in wide shots with a slimmer double, and in close-up was filmed in deep shadow to hide how fat he actually was. Coppola was so fed up with his star's selfish behaviour that he left the set, letting his assistant direct Brando's final shot.

After that, Brando's Hollywood career was largely squandered, taking big cheques for easy work in cameo performances, most notably as Superman's father in the 1978 film – for which he was paid $3.7 million plus 11.75 per cent of the gross profits for 13 days' work, a record at the time.

Above: Elizabeth Taylor and Montgomery Clift in *A Place in the Sun* (1951). In 1956 Clift crashed his car and suffered facial lacerations. After surgery, he developed an addiction to painkillers.

Brando, it seemed, simply didn't care about movies. He took the money, he lived partly on an atoll in Polynesia that he owned, and he overate, by the mid-1990s weighing more than 21 stone (136kg). While flashes of his ability could still occasionally be seen in his infrequent film roles, he treated Hollywood with disdain.

Montgomery Clift

'The only time I was ever really afraid as an actor was that first scene with Montgomery Clift,' said Burt Lancaster about making *From Here to Eternity* (1953). 'I was afraid he was going to blow me right off the screen.' And at that time, Lancaster was the big star, in the big-star role, and Clift the newcomer. Clift, however, didn't become a huge star. Firstly, that was because he could afford to be picky about his roles. 'Monty could've been the biggest star in the world if he'd made more movies,' said his friend Elizabeth Taylor. And, secondly, because he wasn't well enough. In 1956, he crashed his car on leaving a party at Taylor's house. He required major plastic surgery and the pain from his injuries led him to rely on alcohol and painkillers, as he had done after an earlier bout of dysentery left him with chronic intestinal problems. This led to an addiction which culminated in a fatal heart attack ten years later.

Natalie Wood

But what about child stars? Natalie Wood found fame when she was nine with the release of *Miracle on 34th Street* (1947), and worked in film and television, before successfully, unlike many child actors, making the transition to more grown-up work at 16 with her role in *Rebel Without a Cause*.

Below: James Dean (left) looks on while director Nicholas Ray (hands on hips) smiles at Natalie Wood (back to camera) on the set of *Rebel Without A Cause*. At the time the 43-year-old director was having an affair with the 16-year-old actress.

> That Natalie Wood was only 16 didn't stop her 43-year-old director Nicholas Ray from beginning a relationship with her.

In the eyes of Californian law, Wood was still a child and was required to be tutored for three hours a day until she was 18. But that didn't stop the 43-year-old director of the movie, Nicholas Ray, from beginning a relationship with her during the making of the film. (Ray's former wife Gloria Grahame had, of course, earlier been sleeping with his 13-year-old son from his first marriage.)

Natalie Wood's mother, along with the cast, was aware of the relationship with the director, but when she made a complaint to the studio, it was regarding Wood's simultaneous romance with 19-year-old co-star Dennis Hopper rather than the director, and it was Hopper who was told to cool off. Like many relationships that take place while films are being made, Natalie Wood's relationship with her director was finished by the time the movie was released.

Judy Garland

The problem with child stars is that they stop being children so quickly. After working in vaudeville, Judy Garland arrived in Hollywood in the early 1930s when she was already 12, which didn't leave much childhood in her. Nevertheless, MGM's Howard Strickling put her on a diet of soup and cottage cheese to try to stall

Below: Judy Garland was 16 when she played Dorothy in *The Wizard of Oz*. In an effort to keep their child star a child, MGM painfully trussed up Garland's breasts and put her on a diet to stall her physical development.

her growth. When she played Dorothy in *The Wizard of Oz,* Garland was 16 and her breasts had to be painfully trussed up to make her appear childlike.

Apart from trying to hide her sexuality, MGM treated the actress's already fragile nature by feeding her a cocktail of pills – uppers to keep her alert for shooting, followed by downers in the evening to overcome the uppers. By 1940 she was an amphetamine addict.

The studio also spied on her. Betty Asher, an MGM publicist, was assigned to befriend the star, soon becoming Garland's confidante, assistant and lover. In addition to her pills addiction, Garland also began drinking. A nervous breakdown followed and she was unable to complete a movie. Even when supposedly in better health, she was repeatedly late or didn't appear on set. By 1950, MGM had had enough and fired the 28-year-old star. In response, she attempted to slash her throat, Strickling having to pull in celebrity journalist Hedda Hopper to write that it was only a minor scratch. Other journalists, however, were on to the story and it became front-page news.

After leaving MGM, she made *A Star Is Born*

Right: Elizabeth Taylor as Cleopatra. At 16, Taylor had wanted to leave film-making but her mother had said that it was her responsibility to Hollywood to continue working.

for Warner Bros in 1953, but didn't work again in Hollywood until 1958. Later her addictions lead to tardiness and incoherence in some of her stage performances and she was sometimes heckled and booed by audiences. In 1969, she died from a barbiturates overdose.

Elizabeth Taylor

Elizabeth Taylor became a child star at 12 in *National Velvet,* but by the time she was 16 she told her parents she wanted to leave Hollywood behind and have a normal childhood. 'You have a responsibility,' replied her mother Sara Taylor. 'Not just to this family, but to the country now, and the whole world.' Taylor remained an actress, but in later life would become friends with Michael Jackson, who, like Taylor and Garland, complained that early stardom had robbed him of his childhood.

Still, Taylor made the successful move to adult actress, matching Brando's $1 million fee when she was hired for *Cleopatra* (1963). Marrying eight times to seven men (she married Richard Burton twice), in 1983 she admitted to having been addicted to sleeping pills and painkillers for 35 years, and was treated for alcoholism and prescription drug addiction.

Jackie Coogan

Today all Hollywood child actors have reason to thank Jackie Coogan. Best known in later years as Uncle Fester in the 1960s TV series *The Addams Family*, Coogan had been a child star in the silent era, playing Charlie Chaplin's child sidekick in *The Kid* (1921). Although Coogan earned more than $3 million as a

Below: Child actor Jackie Coogan with his mother and father (right) in 1922. Sixteen years later he took his mother to court after she'd spent the $3 million that he'd earned. She denied any fault.

boy, his mother and stepfather spent the money on their own luxuries. So, in 1938, when Coogan was 24, he sued them. 'No promises were ever made to give Jackie anything,' said his mother. 'Every dollar a kid earns before he is 21 belongs to his parents.'

After deductions for legal expenses, Coogan received only $126,000 from the suit. But his case led to the introduction in the following year of the California Child Actors Bill – also dubbed the Coogan Bill – in which 15 per cent of a child actor's earnings must be protected in a trust by the employer.

Bobby Driscoll

Bobby Driscoll had been a Walt Disney child star in films such as *Treasure Island* (1950), but his career faded when he reached his teenage years, and, losing his way, he was soon doing heroin and marijuana. Pursuing fine art, he joined Andy Warhol's Factory in New York in 1965, but left a couple of years later penniless. In March 1968, some months after he was last seen, his body was found in a deserted tenement. He'd died from a heart attack caused by long-term drug addiction, but the body then remained unidentified for a year. As a child star, Driscoll's face was known across America. When he died, aged 30, no one missed him.

Macaulay Culkin

Today's child stars are paid more, and, free from supervision by the studios, are often vulnerable to the temptations of the idle young and rich. Macaulay Culkin shot to fame as the ten-year-old star of *Home Alone* in 1990 and retired as a millionaire four years later. What to do next? While he began acting again in his early twenties, it was in smaller roles in smaller movies. And when not acting? He was arrested for possession of marijuana and two prescription drugs, receiving a suspended prison sentence, while in 2012 photographs of him looking skeletal were followed by worried rumours. By 2013, however, he seemed to be in better health as he accompanied musician friends on tour, while also writing and running an art collective. Perhaps he had found a new purpose in life.

Left: *Home Alone* star Macaulay Culkin retired from movies as a millionaire when he was only 14. In his twenties, he received a suspended prison sentence for drug possession. He now runs an art collective.

Above: Drew Barrymore became a child star in *E.T.* in 1982. While her teenage years were marked by more than one spell in rehab, by her twenties she'd become a successful comedy actress.

Drew Barrymore

Having become famous when she was seven with the release of *E.T.* (1982), Drew Barrymore was smoking cigarettes at nine, drinking alcohol at 11, smoking

> Macaulay Culkin was arrested for possession of marijuana and two prescription drugs, while in 2012 photographs of him looking skeletal were followed by worried rumours.

marijuana at 12 and snorting cocaine at 13. Even when still a little girl, her stardom gained her admission to the Studio 54 nightclub. Rehab was followed by a suicide attempt and a further spell in rehab, while her first two marriages didn't last more than 12 months *put together.* However, having grown up quickly, in her twenties her career stabilized and she became a successful romantic comedy actress and producer of the *Charlie's Angels* films.

'You can't do this to me, I'm Kirk Douglas's son.' A voice in the crowd quickly shouted out, and, in reference to the 'I'm Spartacus' scene from Kirk Douglas's 1960 movie, said: 'No, *I'm* Kirk Douglas's son.'

Stars' Children

There's a story that when Kirk Douglas's son Eric was trying to make it as a stand-up comedian in the 1990s, he became exasperated with his unresponsive audience one night and said: 'You can't do this to me, I'm Kirk Douglas's son.' A voice in the crowd quickly shouted out, and, in reference to the 'I'm Spartacus' scene from Kirk Douglas's 1960 movie, said: 'No, *I'm* Kirk Douglas's son.' He was soon followed by many members of the audience, all announcing that each was Kirk Douglas's son.

One hopes that Eric Douglas took the heckle in good spirit, but he never really succeeded as a comedian or as an actor, which he also tried. His life was beset by drugs and arrests, his father saying that he and his wife had taken Eric to rehab 20 times, but nothing had helped. He died from an accidental drug overdose in 2004.

Eric's half-brother Michael Douglas managed to escape his father's shadow and become a star and a producer in his own right, but Michael's own son Cameron was caught dealing cocaine and in

Right: Kirk Douglas (centre) with his sons in 1987. Left to right: Peter and Joel, both producers, Michael, actor and producer, and Eric, who died of an accidental drug overdose in 2004.

Left: Occasional parent Orson Welles with his daughter Christopher in 1952. Years later a friend of Orson's told her: 'He said that even though he hadn't been a good father to you, you'd been a very good daughter to him.'

possession of heroin. On Cameron's sentencing, Michael Douglas blamed himself as a bad parent for his son's problems, adding that without prison, Cameron 'was going to be dead or somebody was gonna kill him'. But progress wasn't quick: in 2013, having served three years, Cameron's sentence was extended by another three years after he was found to have taken drugs in prison.

> Smoking marijuana intensively as a teenager, Carrie Fisher moved on to hallucinogens and painkillers while making the *Star Wars* films.

In the Star's Shadow

Apart from talent and luck, actors become stars by being dedicated to themselves and their peripatetic job, which might not leave much time for their families – 'An actor's a guy, who, if you ain't talking about him, ain't listening,' said Marlon Brando in 1956. At school, Orson Welles's daughter, Christopher, yes, his *daughter* Christopher, refused requests from classmates for her father's autograph, not out of unwillingness, but, as she wrote, 'because I had no idea when I would see my father again'. Married decades later, it was still five years before Welles met her husband, whom Welles talked at rather than with, telling anecdotes, as his daughter remembered, 'that we'd heard before – with greater aplomb – on television'.

Coming from a world where her mother was actress Debbie Reynolds, her father was singer Eddie Fisher and her mother's best friend was Elizabeth Taylor – for whom Fisher subsequently left Reynolds – Carrie Fisher's path into movies may not have been difficult, but her journey through life was troubled. From smoking marijuana intensively as a teenager, she moved on to hallucinogens and painkillers while making the first *Star Wars* films, before being diagnosed as suffering from bipolar disorder. However, she used her mental ill health, experiences

DRUG OVERDOSES

WHILE HE'D BEEN a popular actor in the 1940s, Alan Ladd's career had waned by the late 1950s and in 1962 he shot himself in the chest. He survived, but just over a year later, aged 50, he was found dead from an overdose of alcohol and three other drugs. Although his death was ruled as accidental, the suspicion of suicide lingered.

Many overdoses *are* simply accidental. Dorothy Dandridge, the first African-American actress to be nominated for a Best Actress Oscar, died from a pills overdose in 1965, aged 42, while 33-year-old John Belushi died in 1982 from injecting cocaine and heroin.

River Phoenix, a former child star, collapsed, aged 23, outside LA's Viper Room nightclub with a heart attack brought on by heroin abuse. Heath Ledger died, aged 28, in 2008 from an overdose of prescription pills, some of which had not been prescribed by his doctors. Having been a drinker and taken heroin in his early 20s, actor Philip Seymour Hoffman went into rehab and was clean for many years, before relapsing and dying from a drug overdose in 2014, aged 46.

of electroconvulsive therapy, Hollywood upbringing and drug taking as raw material for a successful second career as a witty, candid writer. Having reprised her role in the *Star Wars* films in 2015, the following year she suffered a heart attack on a flight to Los Angeles and died, aged 60, days later.

Marlon Brando, despite his obesity, lived until he was 80, but two of his 15 children didn't see 50. In a drunken row at Brando's LA home in 1990, his son Christian shot dead Dag Drollet, the boyfriend of Christian's half-sister Cheyenne. Then, while Christian was serving a prison sentence for manslaughter, Cheyenne lost custody of her child by Drollet and committed suicide, aged 25. Having been released from prison, Christian Brando later pleaded no contest to charges of spousal abuse of his wife Deborah Presley. He was placed on probation and ordered to alcohol and drug rehab. He died of pneumonia in 2008, aged 49.

> Garbo understood what was being implied and rather than getting any older on screen, retired from acting after that film. She was 36.

Below: Marlon Brando and his son Christian Brando in court in 1990. Christian later served a prison sentence for drunkenly shooting dead his half-sister's boyfriend, Dag Drollet.

Body Beautiful

One day during the filming of *Two-Faced Woman* (1941), its star, Greta Garbo, saw some of the footage they'd already shot. 'What on earth is the matter with Joseph [Ruttenberg, the movie's cameraman]?' she said. 'He makes me look so awful!' After a pause, someone said: 'Well, Greta, Joseph's getting older, you know...' It seems Garbo understood what was being implied and rather than getting any older on screen, retired from acting after that film. She was 36. As Ava Gardner said: 'Actors get older, actresses get old.'

Above: Following success in silent movies in Sweden in the 1920s, Greta Garbo moved to Hollywood, although at first she spoke no English. There she was a star of silent, and, later, talking pictures, but retired at 36 before her status waned.

Cinema is a cruel business that celebrates youthful beauty. Anne Baxter signed with David O. Selznick at 17, and made more than 40 films in 20 years, being nominated for an Oscar for *All About Eve* in 1950. 'Those years between 35 and 45 which should be the filet mignon of one's life are a "no woman's land",' she said. Baxter kept working, but in smaller roles and in television.

Baxter's experience remains true today. Major roles for women still dwindle when stars hit their forties, so it's understandable that when they have their faces

'Those years between 35 and 45 are a "no woman's land",' said Anne Baxter. And still today, major roles for women dwindle when stars hit their forties.

projected on to vast cinema screens around the world, they want to look their best.

But while the general public may want to look like movie stars, many movie stars *themselves* don't naturally look like movie stars.

Below: Patrick Swayze and Jennifer Grey in *Dirty Dancing*. A few years after the film had established her, Grey had a nose job that left her unrecognizable – even to friends.

JEAN SEBERG AND THE FBI'S DIRTY TRICKS

BEST KNOWN FOR her roles in Jean-Luc Godard's *À bout de souffle* (*Breathless* – 1960) and *Bonjour Tristesse* (1958), Jean Seberg became a target for the FBI's counter-intelligence programme in the late 1960s because of her support for the Black Panther Party. Estimating that she'd given $10,500 to the Black Panthers, the FBI tapped her phone. Then, when she was pregnant with her second child in May 1970, they leaked a smear story that African-American Black Panther Hakim Abdullah Jamal was the child's father rather than Seberg's husband Romain Gary, a French writer and diplomat of Lithuanian Jewish origin. In the words of the FBI documents, the aim was to 'cause her embarrassment and serve to cheapen her image with the general public'. That August, Seberg gave birth prematurely to a baby girl, who died two days later. To prove that the child was not mixed race, Seberg held an open-casket funeral and she and Gary (pictured with Seberg) later successfully sued *Newsweek* magazine for libel.

In August 1979, Seberg, then 40 and living in Paris, committed suicide with an overdose of barbiturates and alcohol. After her death, Romain Gary said that every August, around the time of the death of her daughter, she'd tried to commit suicide. In response to her death, the FBI released documents admitting their role in trying to smear her name, but stated that such tactics were a thing of the past. 'We are out of that business forever,' said FBI Director William H. Webster.

Enter the surgeon's knife. When it comes to plastic surgery, it might be easier to say which actresses don't appear to have had rhinoplasty – it being suggested that many leading Hollywood actresses, from Angelina Jolie to Nicole Kidman to Gwyneth Paltrow to Halle Berry to Jennifer Aniston and Scarlett Johansson have all had nose jobs – generally quite slight adjustments to give them narrower, less bulbous noses. Among the men, it's believed that Tom Cruise, Ryan Gosling and John Cusack have all had plastic surgery on their noses. Then there's Botox to keep the skin wrinkle-free into their forties and injections to plump up lips.

Unfortunately, we notice plastic surgery when it goes wrong, such as Meg Ryan's trout pout or Jennifer Grey's nose job. Best known for starring in *Dirty Dancing* (1987), Grey was a pretty actress with a distinctive, some might say big, nose when, rather oddly given that she was already successful, she had a nose job, giving herself not only a cute nose like so many other actresses in Hollywood, but making her unrecognizable even to close friends. 'I went in the operating room a celebrity – and came out anonymous,' she later said. 'It was like being in a witness protection program.' She no longer looked like 'That girl in *Dirty Dancing*' and, despite a second operation rectifying the damage done by the first, her career stalled.

> 'I went in the operating room a celebrity – and came out anonymous … it was like being in a witness protection program.'

Plastic surgery isn't something new to Hollywood. Rita Hayworth had her hairline raised and Marilyn Monroe had a slight overbite corrected and her nose pinched. In earlier days, with less sophisticated technology, the surgeons may have been less adventurous and done better jobs. The pre-surgery teenage Monroe was a pin-up, but the Hollywood Monroe was a star.

The Scientology of Tom Cruise

He's been married to three actresses, but Tom Cruise has still been subject to speculation that he's gay, though when accusations have been made, he has

> Told she'd been selected for a secretive Scientologist project, Nazanin Boniadi was flown to New York, where she was introduced to Cruise. They soon began a relationship.

successfully sued. His married life has also led to some interesting conjectures. How, following his divorce from Nicole Kidman, did he set about finding a new wife? Well, according to journalist Maureen Orth in an article in 2012 in *Vanity Fair* magazine, the Church of Scientology, in which Cruise is a senior member, began auditioning Scientologist actresses to be Cruise's spouse. Among these was Nazanin Boniadi, who was already in a relationship with another Scientologist. That is, until the Church persuaded her to end it by showing confidential material from Scientology files about her boyfriend's misbehaviour.

Told she'd been selected for a secretive Scientologist project, Boniadi was flown to New York, where she was introduced to Cruise. They began a relationship where for three months she was seldom alone with him except when they were in bed. Cut off from her family, not allowed to tell her mother whom she was seeing for part of that time, she had to sign non-disclosure agreements, copies of which she never saw.

For some reason, she seemed to fail the test and the relationship abruptly ended, with Boniadi sent from Cruise's home in LA to Scientology's Florida centre for treatment. Part of her punishment there was to scrub toilets with toothbrushes. While former members support Boniadi's stories, the Church of Scientology itself denies them. And if the Church really had been auditioning Scientologists for the role of Cruise's wife, it seems they gave up. A few months after the relationship with Boniadi ended, Cruise announced his engagement to Katie Holmes, a Roman Catholic.

There is a theory that Tom Cruise and John

Right: It has been claimed that after Tom Cruise's divorce from Nicole Kidman in 2001 (pictured with Cruise), and a subsequent relationship with Penélope Cruz, the Church of Scientology began auditioning among its members for a new wife for the star.

A STAR'S ENTOURAGE

STARS DON'T ONLY add to the cost of a movie in their pay, but also in the perks they demand – trailers and trainers, assistants and personal chefs, preferred make-up, hair and wardrobe stylists. Plus a number of flights home for them all. How much does all this amount to?

'Add a third for the shit,' is a saying from production managers who calculate the nitty-gritty of a film's budget. As much as that. But then we didn't really think that stars look that good on screen without any wholesale effort, did we?

> 'I was in a cult for 34 years,' said former Scientologist Paul Haggis. 'Everyone else could see it. I don't know why I couldn't.'

Travolta, who is also a Scientologist, have never won Oscars because Hollywood is scared of the Church gaining any more power than it already has. Scientology's Hollywood members are major donors and also a wonderful advertisement for the Church – until the relationship sours. When Paul Haggis, who won Oscars for the screenplays for *Million Dollar Baby* (2004) and *Crash* (2005), left Scientology in 2009, he rather undermined the organization's endeavours to call itself a church when he announced: 'I was in a cult for 34 years. Everyone else could see it. I don't know why I couldn't.'

Career Suicides

Twenty-first century teenagers would be hard pressed to believe that Mickey Rourke was a pin-up star in the mid-1980s. So what happened? At the age of 40, he returned to his first love – boxing. The fights,

Left: Mickey Rourke ruined his sex symbol looks by taking up his passion for boxing again, but later reconstructive surgery seemed to make things worse. His new appearance, however, worked in his favour for his lead role in *The Wrestler*.

'It's like I've got a shotgun in my mouth with my finger on the trigger,' Robert Downey Jr told a judge. 'And I like the taste of the gun metal.'

however, led to facial injuries that required extensive reconstructive surgery, remarkably changing his appearance. 'I went to the wrong guy,' he said. He no longer had the looks to play a normal leading-man type, but after a few straight-to-video movies, Rourke's career did revive, allowing him to make a virtue of his oddly reconstructed face in his Oscar-nominated lead role in *The Wrestler* (2008).

Ten years after Mickey Rourke dropped off the radar as an A-list leading man, Robert Downey Jr's career began to fall apart. Feted as an up-and-coming talented actor in the late 1980s and early 1990s, he was then repeatedly arrested on cocaine, heroin and marijuana charges. 'It's like I've got a shotgun in my mouth with my finger on the trigger, and I like the taste of the gun metal,' he explained to one judge. Failing to report for drugs tests, he was sentenced to three years at the California Substance Abuse Treatment Facility and State Prison. After one year he was released and returned to work, but was arrested again in 2001 and returned to rehab.

It seemed Downey Jr might not overcome his addictions or that, even if he did, his career would never fulfil its early promise. But not only did it take off again, by 2012 he was the highest-paid star in Hollywood. At first, he struggled – Woody Allen was unable to cast Downey Jr in 2004 because no one would insure him – but, little by little, things picked up, and respected supporting roles were followed by his surprise casting as Marvel Comics' superhero in *Iron Man* in 2008. With *Iron Man* sequels and another hit franchise in the *Sherlock Holmes* films, Downey Jr, according to *Forbes* magazine, made $75 million (£49 million) in 2012.

The Egos Have Landed

Movie stars play heroic roles, but becoming accustomed to being pampered by their entourages and their industry, can, at times, make them behave most unheroically. Writer David Mamet has compared movie stars to two-year-olds: 'a being imagining itself to have vast power, and ignorant of responsibility, enraged by the least human noncompliance as with the broken top that refuses to spin.'

If stars want to take the morning off shooting, they can; if they sense that their trailer is smaller than their co-star's, they're not too ashamed to be seen pulling out their tape measure. If Robert Redford isn't happy, rather than face a confrontation, it is said he'll disappear. Three days before John Travolta began working with Roman Polanski, they had a falling-out, and, before efforts could be made to repair the damage, Travolta quickly left and the project collapsed.

Unlike the rest of us, said screenwriter William Goldman, stars 'live in a world in which no one disagrees with them'. And Hollywood lets them get away with bad behaviour because even if the star costs a great deal and their tantrums, sulks or whims add to the budget, they're still usually worth the investment. With a star playing on his star strengths – Tom Cruise

Unlike the rest of us, said screenwriter William Goldman, stars 'live in a world in which no one disagrees with them'.

in an action role, Ben Stiller in a comedy, not vice versa – they can guarantee that a film will make more of a splash in its opening weekend, that foreign markets will buy the movie, that distributors will invest in it and that the Press will pay attention. The film may not turn out to be a hit, but the star's presence increases its chances.

When Charlie Chaplin, Mary Pickford, Douglas Fairbanks and D.W. Griffith set up their own studio, United Artists, in 1919, Metro's Richard Rowland said that the lunatics had taken over the asylum. Today's stars don't have their own studios: they don't need to. Unlike the big names under the studio system, they are immensely wealthy, and, not locked into long-term contracts, can instead make massive demands that the studios will indulge. They may be mad and maddening to work with sometimes, but on screen they can be magic.

JOHNNY DEPP AND AMBER HEARD

WHEN JOHNNY DEPP and Amber Heard finalized their divorce in 2017, their joint statement said that their relationship had been 'intensely passionate and at times volatile, but always bound by love'. The following year, *The Sun* ran a headline calling Depp a 'wife beater'. Depp sued for libel. Taking legal action like this runs the risk – particularly if you lose the case – of amplifying something that might otherwise be easily forgotten by the public.

At the trial in London in 2020, Depp admitted that, during his marriage to Heard, he had at times had an opioid and alcohol addiction, as well as taking cocaine and ecstasy. Ultimately, he lost the libel case; the description of 'wife beater' was found to be 'substantially true'. He was quickly replaced in J. K. Rowling's third *Fantastic Beasts* film, a recurring role that he'd have kept if he hadn't sued in the first place – or had won the case.

Depp did later win a defamation case against Heard, following an article that she'd written in *The Washington Post*; while, counter-suing, Heard won a single count of defamation against her former husband. 'The jury gave me my life back,' Depp announced when all the verdicts were complete. 'I am truly humbled.' Professionally, though, his lucrative run in five *Pirates of the Caribbean* films had run its course, he'd lost his villainous role in the *Fantastic Beasts* movies and none of his more serious dramas in recent years had made much impact critically or commercially. Pushing 60 and past his pretty boy prime, had the court cases been worth what they had cost the star's career?

Below: Johnny Depp and Amber Heard had met on 2011's *The Rum Diary*. In 2018, *Rolling Stone* magazine described Depp as 'bankrupt, isolated and one more mistake away from being blackballed from his industry'.

MODERN HOLLYWOOD

With the passing of the first generation of film-makers, slicker, business-educated money men moved into the studios. But could they balance the equation of Hollywood – making something commercial that is also creative? Where, a century after it was founded, is the power in Tinseltown today? And what might become of Hollywood tomorrow?

◆

'Escapist movies tell you more about a country than political ones.'

When the studios realized in the 1950s that television would pay to show their movies, they no longer regarded it as a threat and embraced it, with Paramount selling off all its pre-1950 films for $10 million. That was a lot of money, but perhaps leasing the libraries rather than selling their assets would have been a better deal in the long run. Classics such as the Marx Brothers' *Duck Soup* (1933) and *Double Indemnity* (1944) are now lost to the studio.

There were other changes in Hollywood, too.

The generations meet: 29-year-old Francis Ford Coppola directs 69-year-old Fred Astaire in Finian's Rainbow in 1968. Where Hollywood studios had once been factories of cinema, when Finian's Rainbow was made, there were no other films shooting on the Warners' lot.

With the first generation of film-makers dying off and ticket sales falling, the studios began to be sold to conglomerates. Where once they'd been in the hands of people who'd begun in movies by operating nickelodeons, they were now divisions of large companies who ran airlines, car-rental and life-insurance businesses. Keener on money than movies and anxious to cut the studios' severe debts, some of the conglomerates sold off more assets, with 20th Century Fox making a quick $43 million with the sale of 180 acres of its back lot for redevelopment. On the day in 1968 when a 22-year-old George Lucas arrived at Warner Bros. to begin an apprenticeship under director Francis Ford Coppola on *Finian's Rainbow*, Jack Warner left the studio for good, having sold the company he'd co-founded in 1918 to a television company. Apart from *Finian's Rainbow*, there were no other films in production on the Warners' lot.

The uncertainty within the studios in the 1960s

did, however, allow a new generation of film-makers to emerge with off-beat and mature films such as *Bonnie & Clyde*, *The Graduate*, *Five Easy Pieces*, *Shampoo* and *Taxi Driver*. Then, in 1973, George Lucas's *American Graffiti* showed that a low-budget film with no stars could become a major hit.

It was *Jaws*, however, released two years later, that really changed things. Problems with the weather and the special effects had pushed the film three times over budget for its 27-year-old director Steven Spielberg, but *Jaws* went on to be a bigger hit than Universal had ever imagined. Then in 1977, George Lucas's *Star Wars* beat *Jaws*'s box-office record. The message seemed to be that younger directors were changing the face of Hollywood. Some were, but not always for the better.

Heaven's Gate

United Artists was doing well in the 1970s from the James Bond and *Rocky* films, but both franchises lacked prestige. Aspiring to make something with greater significance, UA signed up writer-director Michael Cimino, who'd just made *The Deer Hunter* (1978), an Oscar-winning hit about the Vietnam War. Cimino was now in a position to make great demands on his next

> Filming in a remote part of Montana, the cast and crew lost four hours each day just travelling to and from the location.

film, *Heaven's Gate* (1980), a poetic, epic Western. But things quickly began to unravel for both him and UA.

'Cimino was building sets and rebuilding them, hiring 100 extras, then 200, then 500,' Steven Bach, United Artists' head of worldwide productions, later wrote, 'adding horses and wagons and hats, shoes, gloves, dresses, top hats … with hundreds of miles of exposed film.' Filming in a remote part of Montana, the cast and crew lost four hours each day just travelling to and from the location. After 12 days of meticulous shooting, the production was already ten

Below: A single film can bring down a studio. Allowing the movie to go four times over budget, United Artists had hoped that *Heaven's Gate* would be both a blockbuster and a masterpiece. It ended up being neither and bankrupted the studio.

days behind schedule. By the time a fifth of the script had been shot, the perfectionist Cimino had already spent the entire original budget.

Under the old studio system, Cimino would have been replaced long before things got so out of hand, but, as the star director, he'd negotiated himself final cut on the editing and length of the film. Perhaps, the studio must have hoped, *Heaven's Gate* would, like *Jaws*, be a troubled production that still became a landmark Hollywood hit.

Alas, the movie, which ultimately went four times over budget, proved to be an underwhelming drama dressed in a series of beautifully composed images. It hadn't been worth the wait or the cost. It did become a Hollywood landmark, however. Not only did *Heaven's Gate* lose the studio $40 million, it almost bankrupted United Artists. Following this disaster, United Artists was sold to MGM, which effectively ended UA's existence for many years. The studio that had been set up by Charlie Chaplin and others to give them the freedom to make films the way they wanted had been brought down by a director with too much freedom.

The result was that from the 1980s, directors were reined in by the studios, who reasserted themselves. If there were excessive productions, it was the producers, for the most part, who were deemed responsible.

The Monster of Blockbusters

Jaws not only showed how films could make more money, but also how they could cost a great deal more to release. With heavy TV advertising and nationwide releases on the same day, rather than being rolled out slowly across the country, *Jaws* became a major event. This was, however, an expensive and risky approach. If a movie released that way failed at the box office, the studio was saddled with hundreds of prints that soon weren't wanted, and the cost of massive, but fruitless, advertising.

Nevertheless, in hoping to ape the success of *Jaws*, the studios were willing to spend more, directing their focus at children and the 16–24-year-old age groups – youngsters keen to get out of the house. Not that that guaranteed a success. As William Goldman, the screenwriter of *Butch Cassidy and the Sundance Kid,* wrote about Hollywood: 'Nobody knows anything.' No one can predict a flop or a hit. If they could, why was *Raiders of the Lost Ark* turned down by every studio except Paramount?

> No one can predict a flop or a hit. If they could, why was *Raiders of the Lost Ark* turned down by every studio except Paramount?

In trying to secure some guarantee of success, the studios have also increasingly pursued stars. With a star, at least they can say that the film should be popular. And while a hit movie doesn't necessarily follow, the stars can increase their fees, in turn making the movies even more expensive. This gears the studios to releasing star vehicles or special-effects spectaculars

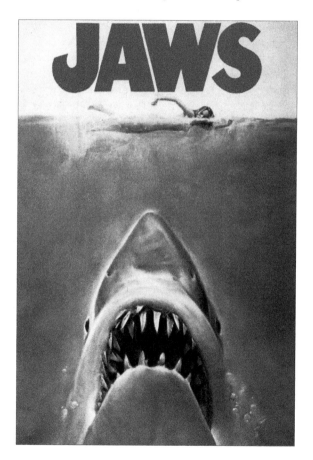

Above: At a test screening of *Jaws*, Steven Spielberg saw a horrified man run from the auditorium and be sick. At first, the director feared the audience hated his film, but when the man returned to his seat, Spielberg knew that he had a hit.

> Don Simpson's drink and cocaine excesses – he'd wrecked his car three times in a year – led to him being fired by Paramount.

– sometimes one and the same – but leaves them less inclined to make cheaper, lower-profile films that would previously have been released slowly and been able to build a following.

Producers

While a criticism of the studio system was that they were factory assembly lines, since the 1970s the allegation has been that Hollywood is now run dispassionately by agents and lawyers who can make great deals, but who haven't made films themselves and don't understand the artistic side of cinema. 'I've had creative meetings,' wrote William Goldman, 'only to realize half an hour in that the producer or executive hasn't read my script at all.' Jon Peters, once a celebrity hairdresser and boyfriend of Barbra Streisand before becoming the producer of *The Color Purple*, *The Witches of Eastwick* and *The Bonfire of the Vanities* – all adapted from novels – even admitted: 'I've never really read a book.' This didn't seem to hinder a very successful producing career or hold Peters back from being given the job co-running Columbia in 1989. That said, within a couple of years he'd been fired, and his time there is considered one of the studio's most financially disastrous.

Don Simpson

Stars and some directors become famous, but not many producers do. In the 1980s, however, as the studios and the producers regained their muscle, some movies were made that could

Right: *An Officer and A Gentleman* became a hit for Richard Gere and Debra Winger, but Gere had turned the script down eight times and the studio hadn't wanted to cast Winger.

be identified by the names of their producers alone. Perhaps the most conspicuous of these, both in his films and personality, was Don Simpson.

Before becoming a producer, Simpson had been head of production at Paramount. He may have been talented, but he was also obnoxious. When he didn't want to cast Debra Winger in a role, he told her: 'I need someone f**kable. You're not f**kable enough for this part.' The film was *An Officer and a Gentleman* (1982), and Simpson was clearly no gentleman – though, despite his reservations, Winger was cast in the role.

Eventually, Simpson's drink and cocaine excesses – he'd wrecked his car three times in a year while under the influence – led to him being fired by Paramount and offered a deal as a producer affiliated to the studio. This was a come-down and a decade later he'd still be known to bring it up: 'They had executives buggering boys in the backseats of their Porsches, and they fired me on a f**king *morals* charge!' Nevertheless, it was as a producer that he made his name. With partner Jerry Bruckheimer, he produced *Flashdance*, *Beverly Hills Cop* and *Top Gun* – glossy, loud and brash stories that were very successful. They also had hit songs on their soundtracks that crossed over well to the

Above: Producers Don Simpson and Jerry Bruckheimer became known for *Flashdance, Beverly Hills Cop* **and** *Top Gun.* **'A series of soundtracks in search of movies' was how another producer described them.**

newly emerging MTV. And, unlike the executives who barely read, Simpson was a producer heavily involved in the development of the scripts he commissioned, once sending Joe Eszterhas a 48-page memo of notes in response to a draft of his *Flashdance* screenplay.

> In the month of July 1995, Simpson had a $12,000 bill from one pharmacy – but he was using at least seven others.

When he wasn't working, Simpson enjoyed a great deal of sadomasochistic sex with prostitutes working for Madam Alex and Heidi Fleiss. In one encounter, according to the book *You'll Never Make Love In This Town Again,* he paid for two prostitutes where one was forced to drink from a toilet bowl into which Simpson was peeing, while the other, a dominatrix with a dildo strapped to her, had sex with the first girl.

Nor did being fired by Paramount curb his drinking or cocaine-snorting. Although there were spells in rehab, by the 1990s he was also on a mix of prescription drugs, while later he began using heroin. In the month of July 1995, he had a $12,000 bill from one pharmacy – but was using at least seven others.

In addition to his drug-taking, his binge-eating and plastic surgery began to make him unrecognizable to friends. He had collagen implants in his chin, lip and cheeks, tummy tucks and liposuction treatments. Nor did he just want to look different, he wanted to feel different, too. He had testosterone injected into his buttocks to increase his sex drive – although it just made him aggressive – and had penis-girth enlargement surgery, which turned out to be a disaster. The fat injections became infected and had to be removed.

It might come as little surprise that he wasn't easy to work with. Assistants could be fired for bringing him

DAVID BEGELMAN

HEADS OF HOLLYWOOD studios are paid handsomely and enjoy generous expense accounts, so it was particularly surprising in 1976 when the president of Columbia, David Begelman, was discovered to have forged the signature on and cashed a $10,000 cheque made out to actor Cliff Robertson. On investigation, it was revealed that Begelman, under whose leadership Columbia's fortunes had revived, had embezzled a further $65,000 from the studio. He was sentenced to community service, and the studio, announcing only that he was suffering 'emotional problems', quietly fired him.

Given his status in Hollywood, he could have easily borrowed the sums – not vast by movie standards – but Begelman had always lived on the edge. When he'd been an agent in the 1960s he'd been sued by his client Judy Garland for money she claimed he owed her, and he was known to gamble heavily. He lied, too. From a modest upbringing in the Bronx, he'd talked up his wartime training on the Yale University campus into having graduated from Yale.

In the early 1980s, he found new work, first as president of MGM, but was unable to repeat the success he'd enjoyed at Columbia, and by the mid-1990s had to declare himself bankrupt. He committed suicide in 1995.

his coffee with the wrong cream, or would be woken in the middle of the night if he wanted them to order him a takeaway – even when he was in a hotel in Hawaii and they were in Los Angeles.

Having increasingly run the Simpson/Bruckheimer show alone while Simpson was absent due to health problems, Bruckheimer broke up their partnership in 1995. A few months later, in January 1996, Simpson died of heart failure brought on by cocaine and prescription drugs.

Simpson's movies weren't passion projects from writers, directors or actors. 'The movie is the auteur,' said Simpson. But it was Simpson and Bruckheimer themselves who left the greatest impression on their films.

Creative Differences

'The trouble with making movies is that it's such an intimate experience,' said Dustin Hoffman. 'You get married when you start working together, before you've become friends.' And those forced marriages, between actors, directors, producers and writers, are often fraught. Take Kirk Douglas, for example, who called his director Stanley Kubrick 'a talented shit'. As actor and producer of *Paths of Glory* and *Spartacus*, Douglas had been impressed with Kubrick's skill, but was riled by the director's later comments knocking the star, disowning *Spartacus*, even though it put him on the A-list, and claiming that Douglas was merely an employee on *Paths of Glory*, when it was Douglas who'd hired Kubrick on both films.

Film is a collaborative business, they say, but for screenwriters, David Mamet feels, the adage should be rendered: 'Film is a collaborative business: bend over.' Having dreamt up a movie, the screenwriter, once money has changed hands, can be, and very often is, fired. If kept on the production, screenwriters will often be asked to ignore their contracts and repeatedly rewrite for no further money, and to revise the script to the demands and whims of the star, director and producer. Daring to resist, a writer can easily be replaced, thus ensuring what he most fears coming true: that although he has caused this movie to be made, he will have absolutely no say in the final version.

> 'To attend one of these script meetings is to understand the cold truth of the saying that a camel is a horse made by a committee.'

Once a script has been commissioned, the studio and producers can only wait until the writer has finished. This, says screenwriter Robert Towne, 'explains the historic hatred Hollywood has always displayed for the screenwriter'. His collaborators feel contempt because they have to wait for the writer, but also fear because they realize they need him.

And, although only cinematographers understand lighting, almost everyone in Hollywood can read. Thus studios will call script conferences with 12 executives and assistants offering their thoughts on a project. 'To attend one of these meetings is to understand the cold truth of the saying that a camel is a horse made by a committee,' said writer John Gregory Dunne. After being harassed with too many opinions, once a film is shooting, the writer often finds himself excluded, needing to be invited to be allowed on set and having to push to remain part of the collaboration.

So it further stings writers when directors elevate their

Left: Film-making can be a testing collaboration. Star and producer Kirk Douglas (right) was both impressed and exasperated by the talent and ego of director Stanley Kubrick (seen here with him on 1957's *Paths of Glory*).

names with the possessive 'a film by ...' credit. The theory that the director is author of the film – the auteur theory – was developed by French critics in the 1950s. It may make just a little more sense in France, where the director often co-writes the screenplay, has final cut over his film and even owns the copyright. But, as William Goldman put it, 'it sure as shit isn't true in Hollywood. I haven't even met a director who believes it'. Nevertheless, almost all Hollywood directors use the possessive credit, some arguing that it's in response to the growing list of producers' names now credited on films.

The director, of course, has his own off-screen dramas to handle. He has to cajole performances out of, at times, temperamental stars, keep filming on schedule and allow the producers and the studio, who often all have different opinions, to believe that the film he is making will be exactly what they imagined. As Billy Wilder said: 'A director must be a policeman, a midwife, a psychoanalyst, a sycophant and a bastard.' But whatever credit directors take, they almost always admit that Alfred Hitchcock was correct when he said: 'There are three things you need to make a good movie: a good script, a good script and a good script.'

Anthony Pellicano

When *Los Angeles Times* journalist Anita Busch returned to her car one day in 2002, she found a rose and a dead fish on the broken windscreen. Attached was a card reading 'STOP'. She contacted the police and an investigation led them to private detective Anthony Pellicano – 'PI to the stars', as he was known.

While searching Pellicano's offices, the police found explosives, two hand grenades and extensive wire-tapping equipment, including a recording of a telephone conversation between Tom Cruise and Nicole Kidman around the time of the break-up of their marriage.

A NIGHT AT THE OSCARS

AT THE ACADEMY Awards in 1983, Polish film-maker Zbigniew Rybczynski (pictured, left) earned the dubious distinction of being the only person to win an Oscar, and, within minutes, be arrested and jailed. On receiving his award for his short animation, Rybczynski, who'd left Poland to seek political asylum in Austria the previous year, tried, through an interpreter, to make a brief political comment in support of Poland's Solidarity movement. Instead, the Academy's orchestra cut in with the Looney Tunes music and Rybczynski was ushered off the stage.

Still holding his Oscar, Rybczynski stepped outside the theatre to smoke a cigarette. When he wanted to return to the ceremony, a security guard refused to allow him in. With Rybczynski protesting, the confrontation escalated and the police were called. Rybczynski, according to the police, was intoxicated and shouted 'American Pig ... I have Oscar', before trying to kick one of them. He was arrested, put in the cells and his Oscar booked as 'property'. In time, a celebrity lawyer and interpreter were found and he was released without charge. Reflecting on his Oscar night, Rybczynski said, 'Success and defeat are quite intertwined.'

It emerged that Pellicano's clients included top agent Michael Ovitz, former manager and Paramount Pictures chief Brad Grey, Hollywood lawyer Bertram Fields and *Die Hard* director John McTiernan. Targets of Pellicano's work were, among others, Sylvester Stallone and Garry Shandling, best known as TV's Larry Sanders.

Grey had hired Pellicano to investigate Shandling, his former client, after Shandling sued him for $100 million for unpaid royalties, while Busch had written a great deal about Ovitz and believed, but never

---

Pellicano was found guilty of racketeering, computer fraud and wire-tapping. But the full stories of his wire-tapping are still unknown.

---

confirmed, that he was behind Pellicano's intimidation of her. Often employed by lawyers, Pellicano's role was to dig up dirt to discredit someone who'd brought a lawsuit. His team included a former LA police sergeant, a computer expert and a former telephone company technician.

Pellicano's clients claimed that they'd been unaware he was using illegal methods, and in court the private detective pleaded the Fifth Amendment rather than incriminate himself, and possibly others. In 2008, he was found guilty of 76 criminal charges, including racketeering, computer fraud and wire-tapping. The full stories of his wire-tapping are still not known.

Whose Idea is it Anyway?

In 1982, *Washington Post* humourist Art Buchwald sold a comedy idea about an African potentate visiting America to Paramount. Buchwald imagined it as a vehicle for Eddie Murphy, who, at that point, was still only a stand-up comedian. After a few scripts were commissioned based on Buchwald's idea, nothing came of it, however, which is usual in Hollywood – 80 per cent of scripts not being made into movies.

In 1986, Buchwald's idea was re-optioned, this time by Warner Bros., but before a movie could be made of it, Paramount announced Eddie Murphy's next film – *Coming to America* – the story of an African prince's experiences in New York. It seemed to Buchwald that

CRUISE CONTROL

WHEN TOM CRUISE fired his publicist Pat Kingsley in 2004, his well-controlled public presence that Kingsley had handled for 14 years began to wobble. Oddest of all was his appearance the following year on the Oprah Winfrey Show when he jumped up and down on the sofa, announcing his new love for Katie Holmes.

So, what had Cruise lost in parting with Kingsley? As stars became more powerful in the 1980s and 1990s, Kingsley and others took control back from the media. She limited the number of interviews that stars gave and would approve the journalists first – *Rolling Stone* magazine once having 14 journalists rejected before one was approved to interview Cruise. Also, journalists wouldn't be given access to a big star of Kingsley's before they'd written fawning articles about a couple of her less well-known clients. All of which is why, today, celebrity interviews risk being little more than froth.

The media, however, can fight back. When Kingsley wouldn't agree to Tom Cruise and Nicole Kidman being interviewed together about their film *Eyes Wide Shut* on the *Today* show, the TV producers refused to have any of Kingsley's other clients on the programme either. And, although interviews may be more rigorously controlled now, celebrity magazines and websites, relying on catty comments, paparazzi photographs and revealing quotes from unnamed insiders, have emerged to fill in the juicier elements about the stars' private lives.

this was his idea, but Murphy was credited as the author of the film's story. It's quite likely that Murphy *was* the sole author of the story – there are scores of ideas and scripts received by studios every day and some are bound to be similar. And the head of production at Paramount who'd optioned Buchwald's idea was no longer at the studio when *Coming to America* was commissioned.

Buchwald, however, brought a suit that Paramount had stolen his idea, and he won. By this point, the

Above: Where there's a hit, there's a writ: journalist Art Buchwald successfully sued Paramount Pictures over the Eddie Murphy comedy *Coming to America*, which he believed was based on an idea he'd earlier offered the studio.

> Rather than be forced to reveal
> their accounting system,
> the studio settled out of court for
> an undisclosed sum.

movie had made $288 million at the box office, so how much would Buchwald receive for his contribution to the hit? Nothing. According to Paramount, they'd spent so much making and marketing the movie that it hadn't yet turned a net profit.

Hundreds of millions at the box office and still no profit? Yes, but rather than be forced to reveal their accounting system after Buchwald threatened to launch an appeal, the studio settled out of court for an undisclosed sum.

'Every movie I have been involved with that was a big hit had people suing the studio saying it was their idea,' said *Coming to America*'s director John Landis, who also made *Animal House*, *The Blues Brothers* and *Trading Places*. 'On *Animal House*, there were four lawsuits and Universal just settled them, as that was cheaper than fighting and even prevailing.' As a consequence, studios, these days, won't even read a script they haven't requested.